The Journey of a West Coast Doctor's Daughter

LOIS MCLEAN HOOKS

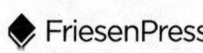
 FriesenPress

Suite 300 - 990 Fort St
Victoria, BC, V8V 3K2
Canada

www.friesenpress.com

Copyright © 2021 by Lois McLean Hooks
First Edition — 2021

All rights reserved.

No part of this publication may be reproduced in any form, or by any means, electronic or mechanical, including photocopying, recording, or any information browsing, storage, or retrieval system, without permission in writing from FriesenPress.

ISBN
978-1-03-911770-9 (Hardcover)
978-1-03-911769-3 (Paperback)
978-1-03-911771-6 (eBook)

1. BIOGRAPHY & AUTOBIOGRAPHY, PERSONAL MEMOIRS

Distributed to the trade by The Ingram Book Company

Table of Contents

Foreword	vii
From the Perspective of a Staff Member	ix
The Blue Cedar-Lined Trunk	1
Esperanza	5
Growing Up at Esperanza	9
Yearly Holidays	15
Christmas at Esperanza	19
The School House	23
Sundays on the Mission	27
My Short-Lived Store	29
Flynn's Cove	33
Prairie	37
God Has a Plan	43
Does God Care?	49
The Sparrow	53
Lois, I'm Holding You	57
Cougars	59
Tahsis Prince	63

My First Catalogue Order	71
The Princess MaQuinna	73
The Messenger lll	75
Hungerford's Anniversary	81
Day Trips to Ferrier Point	85
Dad	93
Mission Ventures	107
Dad's Shipwreck	111
Miracle Stones	115
Percy Wills	121
Friendly Cove	125
Mother	129
A Shoe Story	137
Our Son Grant	139
Kids Say the Funnest Things	147
YOU Are God's Plan	153
"I Will Carry You"	157

Foreword

The other day I was talking to a friend who had been a staff member at Esperanza for many years. I was relating the story of our little dog Spottie, and she said, "That's not how Spottie died." I was surprised. We had another dog or two, and whether she was mixed up with them and their ending, I'm not sure. Many of our pets had their lives ended by cougars. But as for our little dog, his life ended in the way I have described in the book.

Sometimes our perspectives differ. I chatted with my sister about something Dad had done. I thought it was wonderful. She thought it wasn't. We all see things in a different light and each story from a different angle. Some of these episodes, such as in the operating room, have been related to me. I wasn't there. The others were part of my life experiences.

Memories are a wonderful thing. I've read extensively about the Inuit in years gone by. They had an interesting custom. They allowed their small children almost complete freedom to do what they liked, so that as they slept in their winter homes, igloos, the children were up at night pretending hunts, making soup, and having a grand time around the fire as the rest of the family slept on their ice shelves on top of their caribou skins. They stated that by the time an Inuit child was five, they could make a pot of soup and tea for any cold traveller who might pass by.

The reason the Inuit allowed their children this freedom, I've read, is because life in those days was so very difficult even to survive, they wanted the children to at least have some pleasant memories in their later years.

I have enjoyed going back and thinking of those days at Esperanza. Sometimes I've been so engrossed that I forget my responsibilities at the moment. My husband will come in asking about dinner. Dinner? Am I supposed to make dinner? And it's hard to come back to reality.

These are stories in the form of vignettes rather than a chronological relating of life. It is simply memories of growing up on the West Coast with parents who served the communities there, along with some episodes of interest in my own life. It really isn't a biography.

I hope you enjoy the memories I've shared with you in this book. I have really enjoyed putting them down on paper.

Lois

From the Perspective of a Staff Member

I was a staff member at Esperanza for many years and knew the mission well. Friends of mine had given my name to Dr. McLean and he called to invite me to spend the summer months at the mission.

Arrangements were made for me to make the journey via the Messenger 111, the Shantyman mission boat. My friends were supposed to be on the ship with me but she had emergency surgery and wasn't able to make it. So I was the only lady on the boat with eight men and was delegated to make the meals.

One day I was preparing tomato soup for lunch on the ship stove when the boat began to roll in the rough water and my delicious soup landed on the galley floor!

We stopped at the First Nation village of Ahousat near Tofino, B.C. on our way up to Esperanza, to hold a special meeting and do some visiting. We found a home large enough to hold a crowd and made arrangements for the service. We sang and the gospel was preached to the folks that joined us. Every opportunity was taken to tell about salvation.

The next morning we untied the ship from the dock to continue our journey up the West Coast and made our way into Nootka Sound where there was a light house at Friendly Cove, another Native village. The light house keeper was always delighted to have a visit from their friends on the Messenger and the men tied the boat to his dock. He was shocked and overly delighted when I made my appearance from the galley to say hello and I began to wonder if I had made a mistake coming to the isolated coast, if men were this shocked and surprised to see a woman!

We continued up the coast and rounded the last point when lovely Esperanza came into view. It would be my home for at least the summer months. We were warmly welcomed by Dr. and Mrs. McLean and introduced to the staff on the mission. I was shown to my new home, the nurses residence, loving called the "Hen House".

Miss Carlile was the matron of the hospital at the time. She showed me around as it would be my new nursing post. She had a special love for the little Native children, would hold them on her knee and gently rock them.

This began my time at Esperanza. My summer months turned into very happy years. I worked along side Dr. McLean and remember his great compassion for the addicts and drunks. One day he was at Zeballos, a local town, and found a very drunk man laying in his boat covered in his emesis so he beckoned help from some nearby men, wrapped him in a blanket and put him on his boat to bring him back to Esperanza. When he arrived at Esperanza two of the mission men carried him up on a stretcher to the hospital where Dr. McLean ran a warm bath and scrubbed the man from head to toe before he found him a bed. The gospel was shared with the man over the pursuing days and he became a believer. This was not an uncommon occurrence for Dr. McLean. He cared greatly for these people.

In later years when Mrs. McLean was teaching in the school on the hill, Dr. McLean would substitute for his wife if she were unwell. Both Dr. and Mrs. McLean were teachers. Dr. McLean had taught school before he began medicine.

Dr. and Mrs. McLean made the mission a wonderful place to work. Mrs. McLean made it seem like home and I felt it was my home all the years I worked on the mission. Of all the experiences I've had I treasure my time at Esperanza as some of the happiest ones of my life. I never wanted to leave but the hospital closed and life sent me in a different direction.

Cathy Birtles

DEDICATED TO

Mom and Dad who were a lighthouse beaming their light to the folks on the West Coast of Vancouver Island. They were just regular folks simply doing the job God had called them to.

The Blue Cedar-Lined Trunk

The blue, metallic, cedar-lined trunk was filled to the brim, mostly with articles I valued. In it was my lace and pearl wedding gown from our marriage in April of 1969. It was wrapped in blue tissue and safely tucked away in an Eaton's box where it had lain quietly for 17 years, waiting for I'm not sure what. Just memories perhaps. Or maybe for our daughter to wear one day if she wished. Along with the wedding gown was a carefully wrapped package of our "Little Treasure's" finest infant clothes. Some lovingly made by friends, some by relatives, and some by me. Others, just special tiny clothes that carried with them the precious memories of a three-week-old baby girl all bathed and dressed and lovingly laid, sleeping, in the comfortable baby carriage that we placed in the large kitchen, close to where I spent most of my days being a mother of two industrious little boys and now this addition to our family.

My favorite piece of clothing was a tiny, delicate blue dress with bits of lace and a bow. It was somehow a treasure that to this day I have wrapped in blue tissue and have displayed in a small, see-through box that is tied with a gold ribbon bow. There was also a bag of clothes that I kept for when little girls like to dress their dollies – not as special, but still it would be fun for her to remember as she played dress-up with her babies. Besides these items, there were a few hand-me-downs that the children had not yet grown into – not of particular value but would come into use as they grew.

One day several years later, we had moved to the city of Edmonton from Victoria, and along with us came the blue trunk with cedar lining, still carrying the valuable cargo. Christmas was just the day before, and we had made arrangements to drive to Red Deer to meet some Calgary friends for a Boxing Day supper. We had been out on an errand in the morning while Grant, our oldest boy, was delivering his daily *Edmonton Journal* newspaper. Stopping to pick him up around 1 pm, we then braved the winter roads of Calgary Trail South to make our way to Red Deer. At the end of the day, we returned home and noticed lights on in the house. Wondering who had left them on, we went to the back door and were shocked to see the door had been forced open, the frame splintered. Yes, we had had some unwelcome visitors during the few short hours we had been away.

My first reaction was to protect the children from any disturbing sights that might cause them trauma. As we investigated, we found some interesting evidence.

Every bathroom towel, both used and unused, was gone. The only ones they missed were a couple hiding away in the dryer. One picture was taken off the living room wall but its mate left. Of course, the TV and tape deck were gone. Any presents left under the tree were no longer there. Fortunately, I had removed all except for chocolates and the odd ornament. A pan of leftover turkey and ham was still sitting on the counter, cold. It had been taken out of the fridge. They must have left in a hurry and forgotten their supper! As we made our way through the house, down the stairs we saw that our freezer had been emptied except for a package of liver. I guess they liked it about as much as I did! The iron and my husband's toolbox were missing and . . . the cedar-lined, blue metal trunk!

As we went to the now empty spot, there sat the Eaton's box with my wedding gown and the package of precious baby clothes and the play doll clothes I had kept for our daughter – the only three things in the trunk that mattered. How thankful we were! And how the Lord cares about the little, yet big things.

Apparently, they had used the trunk to fill with all the items they wanted from our house and, to make room, they tossed out these items that meant so much to me. Yes, and Grant, then about nine, reported his wallet missing from his downstairs bedroom with all $6. It was a few days later, when I went to turn on the living room light about dusk, that I noticed the lamp table my Uncle Vic had specially made me was gone, lamp and all. The matching lamp by the couch was still there. And several weeks later, we realized our sleeping bags also had vanished that day.

Thankful we were that even though many of our household items were taken, the valuable ones weren't, and no destructive measures had been used. Apparently, whoever it was needed these things for setting up house. The insurance company came through, and we were well reimbursed. On our doorstep one day sat a parcel from Terrace, B.C. It was a set of towels. A friend of my sister Shirl had heard of the invasion and gone shopping for us. Many times even bad things can turn out well, and we can find blessings in them.

So the cedar-lined, blue metal trunk was gone but certainly not the memories it carried. It had been purchased for me by my mother for my going away from home at the early age of 14.

Esperanza

My mother and father, Dr. and Mrs. Herman McLean, had built a hospital and mission on the West Coast of Vancouver Island at Esperanza in the 1930s. They were born and raised on the Prairies. Mom and Dad's families had adjacent farms, so they grew up knowing one another. They married near the end of Dad's medical training and spent their first year of marriage in Brandon, Manitoba, for Dad's internship, where he spent each night on duty at the hospital. Mom lived with his parents in Brandon during this time, which was a little difficult for her. Their first child was born there. After Dad's graduation from medical school, they spent a couple of years in medical practice at Togo, Saskatchewan, before going to Bella Coola, B.C., for eight years.

While they were at Bella Coola, Dad worked in the hospital and would occasionally take horse-packing trips into the wilderness to find and treat the First Nations people who lived in the area. Cliff Kopas of Bella Coola was often mentioned in Dad's reminiscing. The Kopas family lived for years in the valley and were well known by the locals there.

Dad had a guide who took him into the back country, and he tells stories in his writings about experiences with this doctor who expected the horses to obey, just like his expectations of children! Dad also apparently thought all disciplined folk should be up at six in the morning, so the campers were awakened in their tents earlier than they would have liked, much to their dismay.

Mother found the extremes of mountains in the interior of British Columbia a challenge to adapt to, coming from the Prairies. But she often talked of Bella Coola with fondness. She loved the Norwegians, their warmth and hospitality. With her were my older siblings of a family of eight children, but we younger members were not yet on the scene. After eight years at Bella Coola, Dad moved the family to Three Hills, Alberta, where he attended a year of Bible school at Prairie Bible Institute.

Dad and Mom were planning on being missionaries to Africa, so this year of Bible school was in preparation for that adventure and calling. Prairie Bible Institute was a boarding school for high school students as well as Bible school students. It was from here that Dad was called to the West Coast of Vancouver Island by the Shantyman's Christian Association, of which Percy Wills was the Vancouver Island director and where our life and my story begins.

Dad accompanied Percy Wills, at his request, on a boat trip around the island to view the situation of the locals there. Seeing the great need of both medical aid and spiritual instruction, Dad decided that this is where the Lord wanted him to spend his life. Dad chose a spot across from Nootka Island, which is roughly halfway up the west side of Vancouver Island. It was located in between two towns, Zeballos to the north and Tahsis to the south, with many logging camps, Indigenous villages, canneries, and fish reduction plants also in the area. It was a busy spot when my folks moved there. If you go to the area now, although as beautiful as ever, it is far quieter with less activity than the years they worked on the mission and when I grew up.

There were eight children in our family and I was second youngest. Large families weren't the in thing at the time. Mom's and Dad's siblings mostly had one or two children. But Dad felt that God should decide the number, and so even though it was looked at a little askance by those around, they were more than blessed by children who were faithfully dedicated to them in their later years. And people looked very differently at their situation in the later years and spoke of their admiration of such a large and dedicated family.

By the time I came along, the older members of our family were off at school, so I really grew up with two other sisters at home and a vague memory of our youngest brother, who was about ten years older than me.

I met my husband Stan in Victoria, where we were married and had three children born in the Jubilee Hospital. After ten years living in Victoria, we moved to Edmonton, where our children grew up and which they considered to be home. It was after 13 years in Edmonton that we were most happy to return to our home province of British Columbia.

Growing Up at Esperanza

Esperanza was a wonderful place to grow up. We had freedom to wander the length of the village without any worries of danger or mishap. The docks and the hospital were the center of activity, so much of our time was spent around these places. We would go to one dock, where large ships came to tie up at the high government dock to fill the mission's gas and fuel tanks or bring supplies, or simply as a place to tie up for a reprieve from their ocean travel. This particular dock had a gas bar for local communities to fill the tanks of their boats as they passed by.

Other times, we walked over to the west side dock to watch the sea planes landing on the channel and taxiing in to this lower hospital wharf, generally with patients who needed medical care or visitors to the mission. Arriving by seaplane or boat was and still is the only access to Esperanza. Fishing boats tied up at this same dock for a visit, to drop off fish for the mission, for medical assistance, or for a variety of other reasons. The local First Nations residents would come to this dock with their fishing vessels and tie up and sit on the edge of the wharf chatting in their language to one another.

We could go into the hospital whenever we liked but of course we were respectful of the patients and the staff that were involved in their work. It was public access so often staff members or visitors would spend time in the lounge visiting with the nurses or friends or patients. Dad had his office on the lower floor where the kitchen and the dining room were. The unmarried staff members and on-duty nurses had their meals here. Occasionally we would be invited to eat with the staff, but generally our meals were taken at home.

The main floor had a men's ward, an office, two other patient rooms, a children's ward, and a large lounge that looked out over the channel between Nootka Island and Esperanza. The top floor of the hospital had three more patient rooms that looked out over the channel, a nursery, and the operating room.

I remember the hospital smelling of freshly waxed floors as you entered. The brown linoleum shone. The nurses were always busy. You might see some admitted children in the hall or some staff member sitting in the lounge talking to a friend. The nurse had her desk in this lounge, so she would often be there making notations in the patient records.

Dad was usually in his office or up in the OR if he was not out on one of his many trips to the local towns. I don't remember him being in the hallway often unless I was a patient in the hospital. That is when I would hear him coming down the hall in his cheery manner, sometimes singing "Heavenly Sunshine," especially if something wasn't going as planned.

One day I was sitting on the steps of our home that faced the hospital when I saw Dad coming around the corner on his way home for lunch. I watched as he crossed the bridge on this beautiful sunny day in his surgical gown, and as he passed me on the steps, he smelled of ether.

As I grew older, there were times I was able to help the nurses make afternoon refreshments for the patients. There was a little nook on the main floor that was called the diet kitchen. I watched them measure out the meds for various patients, explaining to me the habit of checking your meds with the patient name three times to be sure each received the right medication. Generally it was juice and tea biscuits that was the refreshment, and they allowed me to take it into the patients in their rooms.

Sometimes I helped feed the little First Nations children in their ward. They were so cute with their little noses turning up to indicate "no" or their eyebrows gently lifting for "yes." Sometimes it was so discreet that we would ask the same question over and over, wondering why they weren't responding until we realized their little eyebrows were just barely lifting to indicate "yes". These little ones were generally covered in a purple topical medicine for the treatment of impetigo upon arrival. They'd be walking around the hospital corridor with all exposed skin covered in purple.

Lois on her Dad's boat, The Bruce McLean, named after her brother who drowned in a shipwreck.

I enjoyed the medical atmosphere and thought a small hospital was so interesting. You had a great variety of cases, from general illness to broken bones to maternity patients to accidents and emergencies to surgeries of every kind, as opposed to working on a floor of a large hospital where it was dedicated to one aspect of medicine. I always wished to nurse but life took a different turn and I ended up going to the University of Victoria to study education.

We knew everyone on the mission, and everyone was your friend. The locals that came for a visit were familiar as well. We didn't have to walk far to meet a mission man coming across the bridge to attend to the gas pump for a speedboat or fishing boat that had come in for gas. The bridge crossed a little river that separated our home from the hospital and provided fresh water for our use. Or maybe we'd meet a nurse coming off duty from the hospital. The night nurses had a little shack behind our neighbour's home back in the forest so her sleep wouldn't be disturbed by the daily activities of the mission. Or we'd see a visitor to the hospital or maybe a local First Nations person walking by the hospital and our home on the way to the hotel next door. There was always someone around. In the summer, we had many Bible school students who came for experience on a mission before embarking to a foreign field. Many of them went out around the world as missionaries and had gotten valuable experience at Esperanza. Folks from the outside often commented on the isolation of the coast, and although it was isolated, we really were in contact with hundreds of folks from the outside world.

There were few organized activities for kids, outside of school.

So we made our own entertainment. One time my tomboy sister in her blue jean coveralls decided to build a tree house in the woods in front of our home. She somehow secured the foundation to the large limbs of an evergreen tree and was working away at it when the other kids on the mission joined in. We had to make our way out on the thick branches trying to keep our balance while carrying a piece of wood and a hammer to nail it on the wall of the structure. We had a good time working together and enjoyed the resulting little shack that developed. Other times we found ourselves on the rocky beach when the tide was out, turning over the rocks to watch the little crabs scurrying to find cover. Sometimes my brother would fill his pant's pockets with the little squirming critters and come into the house for lunch when a few of them escaped and then Mom was busy running around trying to retrieve them. In the spring Mom asked us to get starfish (now called sea stars) that she could use for fertilizer for the garden. So we would get a pike pole and fish them off the sea bed and bring them to her to place all over her little rock garden on the slope by the creek that ran by our house.

Their brilliant yellow and purple added a lot of color to her garden, and an atrocious smell in a few days! We played games in the woods and a form of hide and seek where you divided the number of kids into two teams. One team would hide and when secured away their team leader would draw in the dirt a general hint as to where the team was hiding without giving too much away. When the opposing team was searching everywhere for the hiders, the team leader of the hiding team would call out pre decided warning signals like blue meant they are getting near or orange that they were far away and so on.

I remember roaming around in my gum boots on rainy winter days when the clouds hung low over the mountains across the channel. It was too dreary to consider taking a boat out for a paddle. It was quiet as everyone was inside out of the weather. There was no activity on the docks, which were soaked with rain. No one was coming across the bridge. It just seemed dreary. So I came back to our cheery warm home where Mom always had the lamps on to brighten dark days and was busy with household chores. We really didn't have a lot of things to do at home after our regular chores were complete. It wasn't like today when kids have a closet full of toys, Legos, and crafts, and of course, there was no internet or television at that time – there still isn't television connection at Esperanza with its isolation – and even radios were heavy with static.

Other times, when the sun was out, how different was my perspective! People were around busily doing their chores. It was beautiful with the blue water highway and the forest green of the island in front of us. Occasionally I sat on the dock on a warm sunny evening dreaming about the city as I looked out over the water. There was something about the silence of the calm ocean that brought nostalgic thoughts of a busy street in downtown Vancouver, imagining folks crossing with the traffic buzzing by. On those sunny days, we climbed into a skiff or canoe and went for a paddle out into the channel. The wind came up every afternoon from the west, so we were careful not to get caught in that.

On one of those calm sunny days, I got into a skiff and rowed out towards the western point by myself. As I paddled leisurely along on the smooth water, a huge whale surfaced right there by my oar. I was so shocked I broke the oar trying to turn the skiff away. The whale just swam calmly by, and I somehow got back to the dock with only one oar.

Mom and Dad never seemed worried about us roaming about the docks or in the skiffs. I never remember them warning us about falling into the water or being careful. We just did what came naturally and had no incident. One might think that our folks might be nervous, especially after losing one son to the ocean. But Mom and Dad trusted that God had a plan, and knowing we were not careless, they left us in His hands.

As a school adventure, the teacher occasionally organized an afternoon hike up the mountain behind the mission. With a group of us, we never feared what we might encounter in the way of animals. The hike was rugged and took us up to rocks that gave us a wonderful view of Esperanza and the channel and Nootka Island across.

We swam off the beach in front of the hospital. The water was so cold it took your breath away, but after a few minutes, you became numb and adjusted to the temperature. We ran and jumped off the dock. Sometimes we swam out and floated over the swells brought about by passing boats. There were octopuses in the vicinity, but they kept clear of the swimmers. One time, a boy from the mission was standing on a log in this swimming spot, and he had a rat on a string. I think his intention was to drown it, but an octopus instantly came and grabbed it off the string dangling in the water.

When it was time to get out of the water to warm up, we wrapped ourselves in a towel and walked home, still blue and numb with cold. It took about half an hour in a warm bath to get our body temperature back to normal. We were so numb we had trouble turning the taps on. My older sister developed a type of arthritis from this extreme cold as she swam for hours.

Occasionally in the summer evenings, some of the staff came out when their work was done and organized a baseball game in the field to the west of the hospital. What fun that was! We loved it. Sometimes a ball would go through a window of the hospital and land in the men's ward that was on that side of the building. All too soon the game was over. How we wished a ball game with the staff occurred more often.

Yearly Holidays

Once a year we took time for summer holidays to the outside world. My older brother tells me rather enviously that he never got to go on summer holidays. He thinks we were quite spoiled! But it could be that the first years on the mission Mom and Dad were simply too busy to take that kind of time off.

It was great excitement for us as kids. We never went for a car ride as there was no room at Esperanza for roads and cars. Boats were always our mode of travel and the way we travelled anywhere we needed to go. With luggage carefully packed by Mom and taken to the dock, we boarded the mission boat and were on our way for the four hour trip to Gold River. From there, a sea plane flew us out to Campbell River, in the days before a road was put through, and we motored or bused to Vancouver. It was an all-day excursion by the time we arrived at our destination, and we were ready for a well-deserved rest.

What fun it was to be in the city with all its busy activity. Our hosts had milk in bottles! Ours came in cans that had to be mixed with water. And chocolate milk! The host of the home would tease us little girls that chocolate milk came from brown cows. The refrigerators full of store-bought city food looked intriguing to us. And sitting by a window in a car, watching the road go by – how different from looking out the windshield of a boat with waves and rugged shoreline passing us.

The Bruce (on bottom) – our family boat. The Messenger 111 and other fishing boats (on top).

One summer holiday trip, we were late starting out from Esperanza, or the seaplane was early. They met us on the way, before we had arrived in Gold River. The pilot spotted our boat en route and landed the plane beside us there in the channel, where we transferred, climbing out of the boat onto the pontoon and up the two steps into the plane. The pilot put our luggage in the rear, and we belted ourselves into the seats before he gunned the engine and the plane sped through the water with a great deal of noise until we lifted up into the air and were on our way. The view as the pilot tilted the plane to avoid the mountains made the ocean appear to be on a slant. Even though flying scared me, it was a beautiful and most intriguing sight. We were always a little nervous of the seaplanes. Watching the pilot do his thing – well, I usually sat with Dad in the back and buried my face in his coat so I didn't have to watch. The air pockets were nerve-wracking too. How many times did we scream and grab the man seated ahead of us when an unexpected one met our plane. Apologies were humbly said and a knowing smile from the poor man and our ride continued – until the next one hit! We were always relieved when the plane landed safely.

We felt somewhat the same about boat travel, knowing the dangers of the coast. It was called the Graveyard of the Pacific for a reason, and many boats went down. The ocean was our highway. There were no lights or road markers. Nights were pitch black, especially if it was raining. A few of the points had lighthouses on them, so you aimed the boat towards it, knowing it signalled the place to turn on your way home. Always we watched for deadheads, logs that stood perpendicular in the water and posed a significant danger if you ran into them. Generally they were just below the surface and showed up only as a wave moved over them. At night, Dad had one hand on the spotlight control in the ceiling of the boat, turning it back and forth over the water to be sure all was clear, as well as keeping an eye on the coastline. When it was extremely foggy, it was the coastline that guided us home, and all eyes were aiding in the watch for dangers on the ocean.

I remember a speedboat that drove right into the side of the mountain east of the mission on a foggy morning. The seriously injured ended up in the hospital for Dad to treat. Fog was only one problem. Low tides were another that you had to consider if you were going to places where there were hidden reefs. Always, wind and heavy seas were another consideration. Sometimes Dad would come home from a trip to the outside water where it's unprotected and say, "It was as flat as a pancake," if the water was calm. I always felt safer on the larger ships like the *Messenger 111,* the Shantyman boat, as the one we generally travelled in was only 21 feet long. I think the fact that Dad was a Prairie son and grew up there, made him take even greater care in his travels on the sea. He was meticulously careful. New staff members unfamiliar with the coast occasionally took unnecessary risks and wound up in trouble. I think lakes to them were similar to the Pacific, but they were vastly different.

One time in later years, my husband and I had gone to Esperanza for a visit and had one of these newer workers driving the inboard speedboat we were in. The water was choppy, but he sped along somewhat carelessly I thought for the condition of the sea, and we landed directly on a log that was hidden in the trough of the waves with a loud crash. Our engine conked out. We sat a minute in shocked silence. Because it hit directly on the keel of the speedboat, we were saved from disaster. Another speedboat was passing in the inlet at the time and stopped to see if we were alright. We restarted the engine and continued on our way to Tahsis where we were headed.

Like many missions in those days, we had "missionary barrels" sent up the coast for those who might be in need. They were very large cylinders filled with used clothing from folks in the city. I remember being with a staff member who was going through it one day in a warm sunny room above the hospital laundry sorting out the items, as I watched. Men's suits. Dresses. Shoes. A variety of fairly good clothing. I watched wondering about the city folks who had sent these articles of clothing up. Did they think we were poor? I didn't feel poor. I don't remember if we wore anything from the barrel. Our clothing came from the Sears or Eaton's catalogue. There was a Co-op store in Zeballos that had shoes and boots and some articles of clothing, but mostly ours was from the catalogue. On occasion, when Dad flew out to Vancouver with a patient or for some other reason, he shopped for Mom and brought lovely quality dresses back for her. His taste was impeccable, and Mom looked wonderful in his choices.

Christmas at Esperanza

Christmases on the mission were a special time for us. Christmas Day was spent at the hospital, so I never remember Mom cooking a turkey. After we opened our stockings in the morning we dressed and went to the hospital for the day. The hospital cook prepared a turkey and all the trimmings, and everything was delicious. Staff set up tables down the hall of the main floor, dressed them in white linen cloths, and decorated the tables with candles, poinsettias, special napkins, and Christmas crackers at each place. A big tree that had been retrieved from the forest of the mountain behind us was standing in the corner, lit up with lights and sparkling tinsel, draped with garland. The children of the mission drew names, and each brought a wrapped present to put under the tree. How exciting and fun it was. I remember one Christmas that I was very disappointed in my gift. It was a book! *Uncle Tom's Cabin*. I was not excited about reading in those days. I never did read it. However, it was usually fun and the gifts appreciated. After dinner together with the staff and any patients that were able to join us, we played games, sang carols, and finally went home in the evening tired and ready for bed. For the rest of our adult lives, most of our family struggled to adapt to the quietness of a simple family Christmas after spending our lives celebrating Christmas in this way, with so many people.

Tables set up for Christmas in the hospital

Christmas Eve was our family time at home. Mother spent the day making treats. It seemed to us to be the longest day of the year. Of course, our gifts had all been ordered from the catalogue in the fall and delivered on the *Tahsis Prince*, the ship that made deliveries to all the folks on the coast. They were wrapped and ready for under the tree.

The tree was the children's project, and we thought it was beautiful. We hung heavy tinsel on each branch, one at a time and it glistened beautifully in the evening light. One year my older sister and I went down to the dock and found a skiff. We decided to go out to the point west of Esperanza and find a tree rather than the usual out into the woods behind our home. So the two of us climbed into the skiff and off we rowed. When we got to the point, we carefully climbed out, took the rope, and secured it under a rock so we wouldn't lose the boat and then climbed the steep mountain to find our tree. After choosing the best one, we dragged it down the mountainside into the water and tied it to the boat with the rope that held it secure under the rock and dragged it along behind us in the water as we towed it home to the dock.

Mom always invited Miss Parry, the hospital cook, as it was also her birthday on December 24, to join us for Christmas Eve. Mom ensured that a gift was under the tree for her. The lights were turned off and only Christmas lights were on, plus the candles glowing on the table in the kitchen. We sat around the tree and sang Christmas carols. After gifts were opened, we moved to the kitchen to sit around the lovely, decorated table to enjoy the treats that Mom had so lovingly prepared. Pink whipped-cream jello, fruitcake, and homemade buns along with a couple of other selections. When we were finished, we hung our stockings on the colonnade between the kitchen and living room and went to bed, excitedly awaiting the morning. Mom had about three wrapped packages in each stocking, and we were always delighted with her choices.

Generally we had attended some special Christmas programs in the local villages where, of course, Santa always showed up to the festively decorated hall. Our name would be called, and we would walk up to the front, sit on Santa's knee, and receive our gift from him along with a brown paper bag of candy that always included a mandarin orange and a candy cane. At the end of each evening, we walked down to the dock in the chill darkness of a December night and boarded the boat, which Dad drove home. Nights on the ocean were cold, but the engine kept us warm once inside. Occasionally there was a thin layer of ice on the ocean, which posed another danger, especially to a wood-hulled boat.

In our school on the hill, we practised our lines for the upcoming Christmas concert back on the mission. We decorated our room with delight. We hung a sheet on a wire to pull between scenes. The staff came along with our parents to enjoy the efforts of their children. Mom and Dad sat in the audience with faces glowing, always appreciative of our efforts.

The School House

The school at the mission was staffed by the government. Teachers were sent up from the city, and we had quite a variety! My first-grade teacher was a little mentally unstable. As a small girl, I was well behaved and didn't have to worry about being in trouble. But one day, the big boys sitting behind me were talking, so the teacher walked down the aisle with the strap in her hand. Apparently, she didn't want to strap the boys as their parents were on the school board so she hit me over the back with the strap and then walked back to her desk. Of course, it didn't hurt but I didn't understand it. When class was let out, she asked me to stay. Then she called me to her desk and made me promise I wouldn't tell my folks. I of course promised and went directly home and told Mom. Nothing came of it as far as I remember. It hadn't caused any harm.

One of those boys and I became good friends in the later part of elementary school. He teased me continually, and finally one day, Mom said, "Why don't you call him carrot top" to see how he likes being teased. He had bright red hair, and I hadn't thought to tease him back. By that time, he was big, almost six feet tall. We were working together at a project in the classroom when I gave him the nickname. He got down off the shelf where we were decorating for an event, ran out the door, down the stairs, and all the way home in tears! I don't remember him ever teasing me again.

This same boy, when I was in about seventh grade, decided one day as we were studying at our desks alone in the school, that he would come to my desk, lean over me, and give me a kiss. Well, now it was my turn to run out the door and down the hill and home where I went to bed and covered up with the blankets! When Dad heard about the incident and happened to run into the poor guy in the hospital corridor, Dad shocked him with a severe lecture. He never tried that again either!

Our school was a one-room building with a coatroom and two bathrooms, one for the girls and one for the boys. A wall of windows faced down the hill and made it very cheery. It was situated up on the hill behind the hospital and the machine shop where the hospital generator was. We had grade one to grade eight and anywhere from 12 to 15 children. Some were from the mission, and some were from the local villages of CeePeeCee and Hecate where the school boat would go around every morning to pick them up and return them again when school was out.

As children, we knew which teachers were good and which weren't so good. One we had seemed to us to be at least 75 years old and told us stories of the war. We did have some good ones though. About once a year, the school inspector would arrive via seaplane and check things out. He was dressed in a suit and looked very professional. We were always nervous and on our best behaviour.

Occasionally, Dad would be invited to come up to the school after lunch to give us a health lesson. Once he brought some cubes of bread and gave us each one. We were to decide whether it was sweet or sour, and I couldn't decide which it was! Another time he brought up a picture of the human body and gave us an anatomy lesson. Mom taught at the school my last year of eighth grade before I went to Three Hills, Alberta, for high school. Mom had taken teaching as a young person and had completed several refresher courses in the ensuing years.

In first grade, I went through an unusual spell when for some reason baby snakes intrigued me. Usually I was not into unpleasant creepy, crawly creatures. Our teacher was mentally unstable, as I mentioned, and as kids we were well aware. One day coming up the hill from lunch, I found a baby snake and decided to surprise the teacher with it. I found a shoe box and put the snake on her desk with the shoe box over it to keep it in place. When the bell rang for school to begin, we all took our seats and the teacher noticed the box on her desk. Thinking something really special was in it, she paraded around the front of the class and spoke of what wonderful little gift must be under the box. When she lifted it up and found a snake, she shot it across the classroom and her face no longer looked pleasant and sweet! She ordered one of the older boys to pick up the snake and put it outside. I don't remember her ever finding out who had done this dastardly deed.

A few days later, I mentioned to Mom that I had found another baby snake and opened the door of the one-room cottage that one of the single nurses lived in. Mom was horrified and decided we had better get over there right away and try to locate the snake before the nurse came home from her shift. So we opened her door and entered her neat and tidy room, looking in every nook and cranny and drawer. We found it all curled up with her underclothing, sleeping contentedly until Mom took it and threw it out the door.

Sundays on the Mission

Our Sunday services were held in the lounge of the hospital rather than in a separate church building. We never actually had a church building. Chairs were arranged in a semi-circle in the hospital lounge, which looked out over the channel towards Nootka Island. Occasionally a boat would pass by as we sat there singing. A piano stood at the front where Mom would take her seat on the bench and play the hymns and choruses. If patients were well enough, they also joined in, and all the staff along with their children attended.

Every service had an opportunity for testimony time, a time when anyone, including children, could stand up and tell of something in their life they wanted to share. And we children often gave testimonies or requested hymns from the hymn book. It was at one of these meetings that my brother Bruce gave his last testimony, a day or two before his drowning. He quoted Romans 10:9–10: "If thou shalt confess with thy mouth the Lord Jesus and believe in thine heart that God has raised Him from the dead thou shalt be saved." It was a comfort to Mom and Dad to remember that testimony after he was gone.

When it was time for the sermon, any staff member, male or female, brought the message. There was no distinction made. The qualities for speaking required a love for the Lord and the ability to speak. All the staff took a turn, although those with more ease in this situation spoke more often. It was partly a matter of experience and learning thought beneficial. As long as you had a word from the Lord, His word is what mattered. When the service was over, we all went to our homes. As Sundays were Mom's "day off," we made our own sandwiches and ate sometimes out in the woods while watching the birds, never going too far as cougars were always prowling around.

We weren't permitted to play games on Sunday – unless they were "Christian" games, which seemed a bit dull to us. We couldn't look at the catalogue or swim or throw balls, so it was a little boring as children. It seemed that a picnic was about all we were allowed to do. As I grew older, I realized that Mom and Dad were trying to teach us to respect the Lord's day and I appreciated that in later years. And of course in those days, you also went to an evening service where we enjoyed being together and singing and listening to the sermons.

My Short-Lived Store

One day when I was about 12 years old, I found an advertisement in the newspaper where you could order a supply of inventory for a store. As I read about it in Mom and Dad's bedroom, Dad encouraged me to order the material. It arrived one day, and I began to set up a little shop in the basement bedroom, complete with a glassed-in display case. I had greeting cards, boxes of cards, men's ties and handkerchiefs, and a variety of interesting trinkets. The staff would come over on Father's Day or birthdays or other special occasions to see what they could buy from me. I quite enjoyed it. But I never refurbished my supply so when I sold out, my shop keeping experience was over.

We had a small store on an adjacent property that a local family maintained. They were not mission folks, but their children went to the school. To get to the store at first, we had to walk around on the rocky beach, but in order to get around the rocky point the tide had to be out. Later, a trail was made through the woods, which we often took to go to the store, climbing up and over roots of trees and sliding down mossy banks. When we received our weekly allowance of 25 cents, I used 5 cents to buy a wagon wheel. They were so fresh, soft, and delicious. Nothing like the ones you buy today. And much bigger. We enjoyed our weekly outing to the store. The children of this family were our friends, so we often went to their home to spend some time. Their parents were Norwegians, and I remember coffee percolating on the stove and smelling delightful.

The hotel that the government built shortly after Dad arrived to begin his mission hospital was next door to our home. A line of tall evergreen trees divided us, and it was built just up the walkway from the high government dock. It was a beautifully built building with dormer windows on the second floor. The living room was graced with a lovely wooden staircase, and the ceiling had roughly hewed 12-inch beams that stretched across its breadth. French doors led to the outside entrance where I often came to buy a small bag of potato chips for 10 cents. I knocked on the inside door, and the lady of the hotel came and retrieved the chips I requested.

It had a beer parlour, which was the bane of Dad's life. Village folks came to tie up their trawlers or seiners at the dock on the days their government checks arrived in the mail, leaving their children on the boat to fend for themselves while they spent many hours drinking at the parlour. Serious consequences came of this. Occasionally, a child would fall overboard and drown right there by the dock. At other times, we would wake up in the night to find a drunken local in our living room. Dad often made coffee for them and chatted until they were sober enough to leave. Another time, they left the parlour, headed out in their boat in a drunken state, and ran directly into an oncoming ship. The boat sank, and the passengers perished.

The hotel

Dad often prayed about the hotel, that God would intervene in its existence. Not intending any harm to the owners but because of the negative effects it had on the locals. And one day, there was a massive explosion. The hotel furnace blew up, and the lovely hotel burned to the ground. It happened to be the same day that Dad had operated on me, taking out my tonsils. I remember waking up in the hospital room after surgery and seeing large chunks of burning cinders floating all the way from the hotel over the hospital and by my window. Our home, which was next door, was being continually doused with water to keep it from going up in flames too. The paint on the side of our home by the hotel buckled from the heat, but God protected our home and the mission.

We had no way to extinguish fires at Esperanza. Somehow this had been overlooked. An earlier time, the machine shop behind the hospital caught fire. It was near the trees and could have been quite a disaster for all of Esperanza. Each person on the mission, including children, carried tubs of ocean water up from the beach to the burning shop until the flames were extinguished. The patients at that time were transferred to the hotel as a precaution. The fire was put out, and after these incidents, fire hoses were installed to ensure fire safety in the future.

The hotel property was transferred to the mission years later, and a brand new structure was built on the hotel foundation. It included a dining room and hall gymnasium that was very much needed after the hospital closed, for meals and services and has been put to good use all these years as friends come for special organized gatherings.

The hospital too was taken down after many years. It had not been kept up and, with the dampness of the coast, began to deteriorate. A lovely new structure was built on its foundation and was called the McLean Centre. It really was an attractive building that somewhat resembled the hospital in that the lounges were set up facing the channel as the hospital did. Whenever I go back to visit, I reminisce about days gone by looking out on that beautiful scene that we enjoyed for all those years.

Flynn's Cove

There was an island on the way to our camp at Ferrier that had a lovely tiny bay. Ferrier Point was a special spot out on the Pacific that we had camp at each year. This little island on the way to Ferrier was called Centre Island and was originally owned by a couple of brothers who operated a fruit tree farm there. They had built a lovely, white, English-style, two-bedroom home that looked out across the bay. It sat alone for years with no one looking after the grounds or home. Occasionally, we would make our way to Centre Island for a little break from the mission and the heavy load of hospital work for Dad, and stay a night or two in the little white house. The fruit trees were intact on the farm after all the years of neglect, but the surrounding land was overgrown. We would walk down the stone steps to the beach to go for a paddle around the bay. It was a shallow bay, and you could watch the large crabs walking around on the seabed. There was a pathway out to the point that had an old wooden bench set high on the rocks where you could sit and enjoy the ocean view and breezes and the occasional ship that passed by. Our boat had to be anchored, of course, outside the bay so as not be stranded on the beach when the tide went out, but also near enough to be out of the wind and waves of the ocean. We enjoyed a few holidays there and have colorful pictures of us girls in our rowboat. There were jars of very old canned fruit still sitting on the shelf of a sideboard. We never opened them, and whether they were still good after all those years of sitting there, we didn't find out.

In later years, a couple from the Seattle area bought the island. He was a veterinarian who flew his plane up the coast to Alaska to do his business.

They were a lovely couple and became friends with the mission folk. We would visit them, and they often came to Esperanza to visit. There was a second old house in this tiny bay, directly across, somewhat buried in the trees and barely visible. It was built of heavy, old dark timber. The doorways and entrances were low. I think it must have been far older than the little white house across the cove.

One night, the veterinarian had a heart attack and died, right there in the kitchen of the old house. His wife had gone to bed when she heard a thump and came down the old stairs to see what had happened. There on the floor was her husband. He had fallen off the chair he was sitting on by the table and was lying right in the middle of her kitchen. The wife in distress ran to call on the radio phone for help. But no one was answering at that time of the night. She cried in desperation, standing over her husband, asking him why he left her when he knew she didn't want to be there on that isolated island all alone. The next morning, she tried the radio phone again. Some boat far away heard her call and suggested she go out to the point and put a flag out to attract a passing boat. But no one stopped. Finally, Esperanza heard her desperate call, and Mom and Dad along with some other mission folk quickly went down to the *Bruce* and made their way out to Centre Island. They brought her back to our home where Mom had prepared her bedroom to receive her. I remember her sitting up in Mom and Dad's bed sobbing and sobbing, her stomach rumbling so loudly that we heard it from the doorway as we passed by, as she recovered from her awful ordeal.

For many years after, this dear lady came up from Seattle to spend the summers there alone on Centre Island. It became known as Flynn's Cove, after their name. She did a lot of beach combing and made interesting trinkets out of her findings. A seaplane would stop in once a week to bring her supplies and mail. The local First Nations who lived around the island in Nuchatlitz, a beautiful village, often came in their boats for a visit. And of course, several staff members as well as ourselves came to visit her in the quaint old home on the bay.

One day in later years, after I was married, Dad took us out to Flynn's Cove for a visit. It seemed a special treat for us as the mission had always been a working mission with little time for recreation and play when we were younger. But this day, Dad and Mom and my husband and I went to spend the night. Mom and Dad stayed in the old timber house with this lady. But we stayed on the *Bruce*, our family and mission boat, for the night. There was a mattress in the bow of the boat that was our bed. You had to crawl in under the dashboard to get to the bed. The bow shape made for a snug sleep, but being young marrieds, being cozy was not a problem. We crawled under there and were lulled to sleep by the wavelets lapping up against the boat as it was tied up at the dock. In the morning, we woke to otters swimming and playing out around the back of our boat, having a great time breaking barnacles off the submerged logs of the dock, for their breakfast. The boat was damp and cold by morning, so we quickly dressed and stepped out onto the dock and walked up to the old timber building to join Mom and Dad and our dear lady friend for coffee and breakfast.

We really appreciated the time Dad spent taking us places after we were married. Other times, he drove us to the old Ferrier campsite where one time he stopped the boat at some odd island, and we decided to take the skiff down from the roof and row to the beach. It just so happened that we found a Japanese glass ball that day that the Japanese had used years ago to keep their fishing nets afloat. My older brother had found a very large one years earlier, bigger than a basketball, on which he painted a lighthouse. This one we found was more the size of a softball that I have still on my window ledge at home.

Prairie

It was tradition that each family member was sent at some point to the high school in Three Hills, Alberta, the same school that Dad had attended for a year of Bible school. We called it Prairie, short for Prairie Bible Institute. We had our one-room elementary school at Esperanza, but the only high schools were in the nearby company towns of Tahsis and Zeballos. Dad and Mom weren't comfortable with us going there due to the negative influence of the towns. So the trunk that I spoke of earlier had been ordered through the Sears catalogue and had arrived via the freighter that delivered all our goods to the coast. The men of the mission transported my shiny new trunk to our home from the ship, and it was placed in "Shirley's bedroom" at the bottom of the stairs of our home. Over the next weeks, it was filled with all the things a 14-year-old would need for a year away at Prairie: bedding, bedspread, two tan rubber-backed rugs, clothing, a coat for the cold Alberta winters, hangers, pillow, and personal items. When the trunk was full and the time had come to leave, it was again carried down to the dock where the men of the mission now loaded it onto the *U-Chuck* for another long trek down the coast, to Vancouver and off to Three Hills, Alberta. The *U-Chuck* is the ship that came to ply the coast after the *Tahsis Prince* and is still in operation as I write. The trunk's home at Prairie was in "D" dorm, the high school girls dorm, for the three years I attended Prairie Bible Institute, until I returned to a new home in Sidney, B.C., where Mom had decided to begin a new life with us.

The U-Chuck

Leaving home at 14 was a traumatic experience, especially for a young person who had spent their life on a little shelf of land between the mountain and the ocean. Mom had a farewell party for me the evening before, and for the first time in my life, I developed laryngitis. I don't know if it had something to do with unrealized stress over the trauma of leaving home or it was coincidence. Dad gave me a shot of penicillin, and it was relieved for a few hours.

The next morning, bright and early, we had devotions in the living room, and Dad read Psalms 37 before we walked together to the dock to await the *U-Chuck* that would take me on the first leg of my journey to Gold River. It was damp and cold and our faces were tear streaked as we waited and watched as the *U-Chuck* employees let out the gangplank in readiness for passengers to walk aboard. I boarded and waved goodbye as the boat pulled away from the dock and I was off for a year in Alberta. It generally took about four hours depending on how many stops along the way, to arrive at Gold River. From there I boarded a bus to Campbell River and then on down the island to Nanaimo, where I boarded the CPR ferry to Vancouver. My sister Shirl met me there and took me to her home where she kept me a few extra days until my voice cleared up. She didn't want to send me on the train to Calgary with no ability to talk. Of course, this meant I was a few days behind the other students coming from other parts of the country and the world, as many missionary kids also attended Prairie. Again, it was quite a shock to disembark from the train at the tiny desolate station in Three Hills. As I looked around for my ride to the campus, an old, dilapidated car drove up with a broken window and no passenger door handle, and the man driving it stated that he'd been sent to pick me up. We loaded my luggage into the vehicle and off we went to the school. That was the start of three years there at high school.

I was secure in the school with its strict rules and schedule. Obeying was never a challenge to me as it was what was expected as we grew up. I shared my little dorm room with a student from southern Alberta. We made it quite cozy between the two of us.

Prairie was an interesting experience. I often wished I had kept their rule book. When I went there as a new student, I was required to visit the dean's office to have my skirts measured for length. My skirt was to be 14 inches from the floor because I was 5 feet, 5 inches tall. The collars of your tops were not to be lower than the two bones at the bottom of your neck, and sleeveless dresses were not allowed. This was also a requirement for those performing any duties on the platform of the tabernacle, no sleeveless dresses. Modesty was its intent. Included in the rule book was days given when the girls were free to walk into the local town of Three Hills. The opposing days were "boy's days" in town. And we dare not go into town when the boys were there!

Because the student count was around 1,000, mostly Bible school students, we had a huge dining room that accommodated them all. There was a large divide between the girls' and boys' sides. Some of the students called it the Jordan River. We couldn't cross it! I was there the year that they decided to mix the seating. Were we nervous and excited! Sitting beside a man! We practised how a man helped seat you and we were then ready for the big day. I don't remember it being so remarkable after all that fuss!

Each student had student work, or gratis we called it. It was for an hour and a half each day. One year I set tables in the dining room after every meal. I remember setting the tables one day when it was announced that a man had been sent into space in the Saturn 1. Another year I worked in the peeling room with another 10 or 12 students. Girls, of course! We sat around a very large tub, about the size of a bathtub, chatted and peeled potatoes for an hour and a half each day for the next day's meal. On Saturday, because we didn't work on Sundays, we peeled for three hours in the morning.

Even though we were not allowed to mingle with the opposite sex, we all had boyfriends – generally with the help of sisters who lived in our dorm. They would pass messages back and forth.

The tabernacle (the "tab") was also an enormous building that housed the student body as well as locals living in the town and visitors who attended. We were assigned seating as in the dining room – row 13, seat 4, for example. There was a Bible school student sitting behind us who marked our attendance. Many wonderful meetings took place in the tab. L.E. Maxwell, who founded the school in the 1920s, spoke each Sunday morning. Always, they had "special numbers" when musical groups sang in trios or quartets and always dressed alike. There was a 200-voice choir that I was a part of one year.

Every spring and fall, we had conferences that were spectacular. People came from far and wide to attend these special meetings, and we had wonderful outstanding speakers. How moving they were! Often we would find ourselves at the front of the tab responding to a call to rededicate our lives. From that school, many missionaries were trained and sent out across the world. Often, Dad and Percy Wills, the head of the Shantyman's Association, would come to the school in the spring and recruit Bible school students to come to the medical mission on the West Coast, where they would receive training before going to a foreign mission field. Therefore, although we were very isolated on the coast, we met many interesting folks from around the world.

When my first Christmas away from home came, I remember sitting on the bench in front of the piano where I practised each day in the music building. I was crying because I was unable to get home for Christmas. Many local students were able to go home, but my home was just too far away at Esperanza. However, my roommate's parents invited me to their farm in Blackie, Alberta, and I had the most wonderful Christmas. They treated me just like their daughter. Everything my roommate received for Christmas, I did too – a mohair sweater and matching material to sew a skirt – and they sent us off to Calgary with $25 each to buy our first pair of high heels. It was one of the most beautiful Christmases with the family on their farm. I was also invited my second Christmas at Prairie, as we were roommates for another year.

We were on a tight leash at Prairie. Our lives were completely regulated by schedules. The bell rang at 6:00 am in the dorm, and we jumped out of bed, threw on our robes, and walked to the bathroom at the end of the hall where we bumped into other students in the shared facilities. The next bell was at 6:20, when it was supposed we were dressed and ready for the day. Now it was time to sit down in our rooms and have devotions. At 6:50 was the first breakfast bell and by 7:00 you were expected to be sitting at your assigned place in the dining hall. The day proceeded thus. Sundays were a little different. At the breakfast table, we were to make a sandwich out of homemade bread and honey butter. It was a delicious mixture of whipped honey and butter. That was our lunch, which gave the cooks a break. After the morning service, we went to our rooms, ate our lunch, had a nap, which few teenagers enjoy, and were required to write a letter to our parents at home, which we handed in as we entered the dining hall for dinner. I was quite content with this setup, although because Sundays seemed a little boring to me, I began to really dislike them, and that took many years to overcome.

Many of my classmates were missionary kids. Some from Brazil, some from Haiti. Really from all over the world. Being at Prairie was a wonderful experience for me with no negative side effects as one might think with all the controlling rules and regulations. We developed some lifelong friends as well as habits of discipline.

As my older brothers and sisters had gone to the school previously, I had big shoes to fill. I don't think I filled them as was expected. Shirl and Don were outgoing missionary kids. I seemed to be quite different. I was just me. Quiet. Reticent. A little on my own. Those older siblings weren't especially excited about my natural quiet tendencies. They made gentle but obvious comments occasionally. One day in later years, a family friend and mission associate warmly asked me, "Why do you think you are so different from your family? Do you think it's because of your university education?" he asked. Other times people would comment that I was somehow unlike the normal McLean siblings.

I guess the answer is that God has a different plan for each one of us, and whether it seems positive or negative to others, the bottom line is that His plan is the one that matters. No, I don't think it was my university education that made me different. I think I was just born a different sort. It wasn't so popular with my older siblings when I was younger but hopefully it has turned out to be the plan God intended for my life. It was never Mom or Dad that made me feel this way. They were aware that His ways and plans for each individual life is a God-given blessing and encouraged those things that made us special and unique.

My blue, metallic, cedar-lined trunk had a life all of its own. It was with me all the years I spent at the boarding school and then shipped back to B.C., and then again several years later, it ended up in the basement of our home in Edmonton where its story in my life ended with the invasion of our home. How many stories we would hear from that trunk if it could talk. It is gone now, but the memories linger on.

God Has a Plan

When I ponder the early start I had and how God protects, I am quickened to realize that He is in control of each of our lives. And the special moments of our early days and those of our children hold precious and interesting stories.

The mission was well established by the time I came along. The older siblings had been a part of clearing the land and establishing the hospital, whether it was working in the kitchen to make meals or building the two small houses Dad began with, one for he and Mom to live in with their five children and one to house patients. Mom used to tell about coming up to this dreary place in rainy November to a little shack. She of course had come from a lovely home. The windows weren't even installed yet, but she did her best to make it into a cozy nest for her, Dad and the children. The water had to be carried from the creek to wash diapers and clothing. She heated the water in a large pan on the stove. No electricity was available for the first while. She taught the children their school lessons by correspondence courses in a little lean to at the back of the cabin and made meals for the small staff that came up to accommodate Dad in the hospital. For ten years Mom and her family ate their meals with the staff. Dad loved this arrangement but Mom had to coax him into building her a home for the family and he finally conceded. The older siblings were not happy about living in this isolated spot with no organized sports, school, or even any children to befriend. It caused some family disruption, but in the end, they realized their blessings and came to respect Mom and Dad for the sacrifice they made in coming to the island.

So I came along about ten years after the beginning of the mission. The larger hospital and other homes had been built to accommodate the growing staff. Dad decided to send Mom down to Tofino to have me, her seventh child, to be delivered by Dr. Andrew Karsgaard rather than be delivered by himself at Esperanza as he had with my older sister. I was the last baby Dr. Karsgaard delivered before he went overseas as a missionary. There were two special nurses with Mom as she labored, one being Vi Swanson whom Mother so often mentioned as I grew up. She was a wonderful, caring nurse who meant a lot to Mom.

It was coming time for Mom to deliver, but the doctor was in no particular hurry to appear. With much concern and skill, the nurses did all they could to ease Mom, but soon found she and the baby were in trouble. The placenta was coming before the baby, which is a grave danger for both mother and child. Mom was losing a lot of blood and felt that her head was sinking, requesting over and over more pillows.

The doctor finally made an appearance, and the delivery was successful in spite of the circumstances. I was wrapped snugly in a blanket and placed in a dresser drawer due to a shortage of infant cribs, where I began life on the West Coast of Vancouver Island.

Mother stayed the usual ten days in the hospital being cared for by the two wonderful nurses and then returned to Esperanza by boat – I imagine the Princess MaQuinna - with her new baby. It wasn't long though before Mother had trouble producing enough milk and soon she had none. Trying the Carnation canned milk, the alternative in those days to mother's milk, it soon became apparent that I was allergic to it. It didn't take long for a small infant to be in trouble with an inability to digest cow's milk. The story goes that my older sister Shirley used to come in to see her weakening baby sister, and Dad would check regularly too, often wondering how long she would be able to survive in this condition. Almost always they said I was quietly lying there, fussing very little. Dad did everything he could, watching over his little daughter, wondering what God would do with this little life. When my sixth month came, I weighed nine pounds. I had been a normal seven-pound baby at birth. One day, Dad prayed over me lying quietly in my crib, "Lord if you want to take our little one home to be with you, we will accept it and give her to you."

Shortly after that prayer, a lovely Christian lady in the nearby town of Zeballos was going to wean her baby boy born about the same time I was. The next morning, she awoke to find she had more milk than usual, and the Lord said to her, "Why don't you ask Mrs. McLean if she would like you to nurse her baby girl?" So she called Esperanza, the offer was happily accepted, and I began to improve in health immediately.

About this time another lady, Mrs. Manning, a staff member at Esperanza, gave birth to a little baby girl who did not live. It was decided that she would nurse me with the milk she naturally produced for her newborn. It was hoped that it would be a comfort to her. That was just another blessing that helped me, a sickly baby, regain strength. I became much stronger as Mrs. Manning gave her time and milk to me. I never heard but surely hope that feeding and holding and giving life to another baby brought a measure of comfort to her. As a young girl, I thought of this situation and wondered if Mrs. Manning ever had any close ties with me in her heart. One day, as I visited her in the Post Office, I asked her if I could call her Aunt Margaret, but she seemed uncommitted, so I let it go. I do remember being given a pink rose tea set at her passing, which I still have with my china. Whether that was an indication that I meant anything special to her, I can only surmise.

It was about the same time that a family in Victoria, unknown to the McLeans, was having their own saga with the birth of their first baby, a boy, who came into the world three months premature. As serious as a three-month preemie is today, it was even more potentially dangerous in the 1940s. He weighed three pounds and spent the first several months in an incubator in the hospital, with no fingernails or eyebrows or hair. His father was a navy man who was out at sea at his birth. His mother had difficulty carrying boys full-term, and years later, after having given birth to two girls without incident, she carried another boy for about the same length of time and lost him. So it was about 21 years later that the three month preemie was married to Lois who was now teaching elementary school in Qualicum Beach on the island. Isn't it amazing how God leads and looks over us daily with His care?

Memories of birth and the special little ones that come to us have been tucked away in many mothers' hearts. When our daughter Kari Lee was born, we were excited for many reasons. A new baby is always a wonderful miracle. She was a girl, which was a special addition to our two precious boys whom we loved and were proud of, and she completed our family of three that we had hoped for. I remember the first feeding. She was born at 1:50 pm, and at 6:00, I was sitting up in bed waiting for the nurse to bring in my baby. I could hear the babies out in their trolley beds on wheels in the hall all crying, hungry, as one by one they were taken to their moms. Soon the beds were empty and the hall quiet, but my baby hadn't been delivered to me. Upon asking the nurse, she responded, "Oh, your baby is just a few hours old – too young for a feeding!" "Yes", I replied, "I know and I was there when she was born! I would like my baby, please." I soon had my baby in my arms and as I sat there looking into her little round face, I saw my mother in her chin and with a little apprehension wondered if there would be any strain between her and me as there had been between my mother and me in my growing up years. Happily, I don't recall those feelings being present as she grew, and in later years, my Mom and I had a wonderful relationship. Mother gave me a special card and note at Kari Lee's birth simply saying how much she loved me. I think it also had something to do with her remembering the rigours of giving birth, having had eight children of her own. Somehow the note seemed extra tender and special.

A precious memory I had of my second son, Todd, was when he was just a day or two old, holding him in my arms as I sat up on the white sheets of the hospital bed, looking into his little face that usually had a little baby frown, noticing that on the end of his tiny pink tongue was a small white dot. Being the usual concerned mother, I inquired about it to the doctor who said it was of no concern. He was a strong baby boy with husky little bones and especially noticeable were his wide sturdy hands and wrists. His personality was gentle and sweet, and I could see and feel that as I held him that day. He was a dear quiet boy.

Some would ask if we were disappointed that our second baby was a boy. We had hoped to have two boys and one girl and in the order it happened. We were not at all disappointed but most happy with our boys. They add so much interest to life.

Todd was born two days before Prime Minister Pierre Trudeau had his second son, born on Christmas Day, his second son to be born on December 25th. Coincident or induction? So Todd and I spent Christmas 1973 in the Royal Jubilee Hospital in Victoria and had a wonderful memorable time with my sister bringing up a Christmas tree – the only one she could find – a candle tree that to this day, all these years later, is still displayed with our manger scene each year. And plates of goodies brought up, so we didn't miss out on any delicious Christmas baking. Dad brought a small plate of his latest treasure – some homemade brown sugar shortbread. A Scottish flavor, I suppose. Seasonal placemats decorated each hospital dinner tray we received, and company wasn't limited so our four-bed ward was filled to capacity with friends and family. It was a happy time. All the infants came to us on Christmas morning with a little recipe card glued to a paper medicine cup that was attached to their heads with a little elastic around their small chins that read "Merry Christmas, Mommy."

Does God Care?

I must have been around eleven years old when I accompanied Dad one Sunday on a trip to one of the neighbouring Indigenous villages of Queens Cove. Mom prepared egg sandwiches for us to take along even though Sunday was her day off. Queens Cove was to the west of Esperanza around Steamer Point and out almost to the open ocean, tucked away in a cove surrounded by rocky juts of land that flowed down from the mountain into the Pacific Ocean. As we travelled down the inlet, the *Bruce*, which was our mission boat named after my brother who drowned in a shipwreck, gently dipped and rocked in the light swells coming in from the open ocean before us.

The day was bright and beautiful, the wind calm as Queens Cove came into sight. Dad manoeuvred the 21 foot boat around the float dock and jumped out to tie the front and back to the cleats, securing it for the afternoon.

This was just another one of Dad's many trips to the village, and he went about his usual procedure of setting up a sound system that would provide the village with some gospel music and announce his presence.

He placed the record player on the inboard engine cover. It was four foot square and about the same height and made out of a warm colored wood. The phonograph played only one 78 RPM record at a time and had a free-standing needle arm that was placed at the edge of the record to begin the music. He then dug out the megaphone and put it on the roof of the boat, facing the shore where the homes lined the ridge above the beach and where the villagers lived. With everything all set up and ready to go, Dad went inside and placed the needle at the beginning of the record and music began to float over the water and up to the village:

> I would like to tell you what I think of Jesus,
> Since I found in Him a friend so strong and true;
> I would tell you how He changed my life completely.
> He did something that no other friend could do.
>
> No one ever cared for me like Jesus.
> There's no other friend so kind as He;
> No one else could take the sin and darkness from me,
> Oh how much He cared for me.

It was the strong mellow voice of George Beverly Shea. The scene was beautiful – the lovely sunshiny day and the beauty of the rugged rocks met by the blue Pacific with the village set back on the knoll above the gravel beach. The words of the song touched my heart as the music floated up to the homes.

After a few more selections, it was time for Dad to take his black "medical grip," as he called it, and a handful of the Shantyman papers and walked up the float that led to the path along the front of the homes. It was his usual routine, and the folks were familiar with Dr. McLean. He stopped at each home, rapped on the door, and came in for a visit, handing them a paper, chatting easily, and inquiring as to any medical problems that may need attending to. Many times he would open his bag and dig out a syringe, fill it with penicillin, and give a shot to whoever required it. Or some pills that were needed were dispensed from the black bag. Sometimes it was a tooth that needed extraction. Whatever the need, he treated it. When his visits were complete and he'd come to the end of the row of homes, he made his way back down to the boat for the return trip to Esperanza, being sure to embark before dark or any winds that might arise.

I remember another time accompanying Dad to Zeballos when a man from the village came to Dad with a painful tooth. Dad, being accustomed to using all available bodies, asked me, a young girl, to stand behind this man and hold his furry head while Dad extracted the tooth. It was my job to be sure his head didn't move. I can't remember whether this man had any anesthetic or not, but I don't remember any unusually loud moans. With skill and efficiency, the man was freed from his tooth and on his way.

Does Jesus care? Oh, yes He cares! I know He cares. The song still rings in my ears, and the memory of that beautiful day is ready to be relived just by closing my eyes and remembering.

The Sparrow

It was many years later that I had an experience of God's care that George Beverly Shea was singing about.

I was 19 and living at home with Mom and my two sisters. It was a difficult period in my life. Dad was still up the coast at Esperanza, and Mom had decided a few years earlier that she was going to make the break and move lock, stock, and barrel from her thirty-odd year home on the mission to town. After all, Dad was passed retirement but was not ever planning to retire, she suspected. And my youngest sister didn't want to return for her second year of high school to Three Hills, Alberta. She being the youngest, her wishes were taken into consideration, and the move seemed important for this reason also.

So Mom began packing up the house. It was traumatic for me as Esperanza was the only home we had known, and our roots were deep. I had had three years away at Three Hills but coming back to Esperanza was definitely "home."

And I had only one year left of high school. Up until now I had never attended a public school. This move meant that I would not graduate with any of my high school friends. Being unaccustomed to even considering I had a choice, I went along with the change. It didn't occur to me to complain until I was 40 years of age and by then I had graduated! My first year of public school, in a new province as far as high schooling went, and my last year of high school, turned out to be a very difficult experience.

Living back at home with Mom and two sisters was very uncomfortable. I had enjoyed the independent security of a boarding school. I could do my own thing as long as it was within the scheduled guidelines, and I found no difficulty abiding by the many rules at Prairie.

So it was one unusual wintery day in Sidney, B.C., where we had our home on Weiler Avenue. Being in one of my many unhappy states there in that home, I climbed into the wine colored Rambler that was the only family car we had and went for a drive. To where, I didn't know. Just drive around Sidney, maybe along the ocean. Definitely not too far away.

As I drove along by the ocean, I decided to pull over and stop the car by the side of the road. There was an area of access to the snow-covered beach. Snow on the beach, and I was getting out of the car to walk down there! It was fresh, cold, pretty with its light dusting of snow, and definitely something different – walking on the beach in the cold! It was Sunday afternoon, and I was still wearing my high heels from church.

I had only gone a short ways when I thought I saw something small and yellow under a driftwood log. "What is that?" I wondered and took a few more steps closer. A bird? It didn't move as I came near. I bent down to see if it was alright. The bird didn't appear afraid. So I picked it up and saw that it was a small yellow canary. Out here on the beach, under a log, in the cold snow! I couldn't believe it.

I was carrying a small, tan colored suede purse and decided to empty the contents into my pocket, thinking the suede would be warm and a good place to transport the cold canary. Without any resistance, I picked up the bird, put it into my purse, and headed to the car to go home. It was still alive but not in very good shape. At home, we decided to contact the local radio station to see if anyone could tell us about the possibility of a lost pet.

It wasn't very long before the call came. Yes, the little yellow canary had flown from its cage and out the door the night before. Try as they might, they were unable to find their pet. Waking up the next morning to snow on the ground, the fate of the little bird was surely not good, and the owners had given up hope of finding it, let alone finding it alive. How gratefully surprised they were to find that their bird was alive and found in such an unusual spot and circumstance.

The reality of the situation struck me. How strange that anyone would go for a walk on the beach in the snow! But God knew that little bird was there, and He also knew the unhappiness that I was experiencing. He not only cared about the little bird, but He cared infinitely more about me – so much so that He would direct me to the beach to let me know He cares. If He cares that much about that little yellow canary, how much more does He care for Me!

He says that sparrows are not worth very much. But He sees when even one of them falls to the ground. How much more does He care for you than for the sparrows!

As it turns out, sparrows would have great meaning to me throughout other experiences of my life, which I will share later.

Sometimes we are unaware of His presence. Or maybe I should say, often we are not aware of it. Or of the fact that He is guiding us as we go about our daily routine or unusual happenings like going for a walk on the beach in your heels on a snowy wintery day.

Lois, I'm Holding You

As a very young child, I got delirious whenever I had a fever. I remember the strange things I used to see. It seemed sometimes that the room I was in got larger and larger until my sickbed was just a tiny spot in this huge room, somehow frightening me. It happened to me when I was at home. On several occasions, it happened when I was very ill, and Dad had put me in the hospital where he said he could make more money on us than if we were home in bed! Of course, he never put us in there unless it was necessary. Other times I would see bears and cougars coming for me and I would be oh so frightened. Cougars were a reality for us there at Esperanza, being at the base of a densely wooded mountain. They were a very real danger, and we were always frightened coming home across the bridge from the hospital at night.

One afternoon I had a high fever and was lying in my bed in our bedroom at the back of the house. I was seeing bears in my room that were scaring me terribly. I began to call for Mom. "Mom, Mom, please come," I called. It seemed that there was no answer, and the animals were surrounding my bed and getting closer all the time. Again and again I called. And then suddenly I heard Mom's voice, "Lois, I'm holding you," she said.

I opened my eyes and there I was, in Mom's lap. Somewhere along the line, Mom had picked me up and carried me to the living room. I was totally unaware that she had taken me from my scary room, away from the bears, and that I was sitting on her lap in front of the living room window. It wasn't until I heard her voice saying, "Lois, I'm holding you" that I opened my eyes and saw that she was with me and I wasn't alone.

Often I have thought of that in relation to the Lord. He is near, and so often we are not aware of His closeness. Sometimes we are scared to death of a situation, but He is there, holding us. We just need to open our eyes and listen to His voice and remember that He has promised never to leave us. Never, ever.

Cougars

Our neighbours in the government hotel that was next door to our home had two dogs that roamed the area at night. They were beautiful golden labs called Prince and Major. We used to say that one of these days, a cougar is going to get them. And sure enough, one night we heard a ruckus outside and jumped out of bed to see what was going on. As we got to the window, we saw in the darkness one of the dogs roll into the little creek that ran past our house and then we saw a cougar jump into the trees. Our dog in the basement was going wild with barking at the commotion. We called the neighbour from the hotel, and he came over with his gun to look for the cougar but in the darkness he couldn't find it. So he went home.

Dad had been called to the hospital in the night and came home about this time, stopping at the basement door of our house to hush our little dog Spottie. When Dad came upstairs, he was surprised to find us up. We told him the story, so he took the flashlight and went outside in the darkness and into the woods, standing under a slanted tree looking everywhere for the cougar, but he could see no sign of him. So he and the rest of the family went to bed. My sister and I decided to have another look after everyone was gone. She took the flashlight and shone it out the window – directly into the eyes of the cougar. They shone like golden globes looking back at us there in the kitchen. So we called the hotel manager again, and he found the cougar in the tree that Dad had stood directly under, shot him once, and the cougar leaped up in the air and landed on the same branch. He shot again, and the cougar jumped off into the bushes. The next morning, we found him lying dead among the trees. He was a young two-year-old. The dog he attacked disappeared into the woods and showed up several days later with a very swollen face and head but did manage to recover.

Another time Dad was driving the boat to Tahsis in the afternoon when he spotted a cougar come down off the rocks and swim out to his boat. It seemed he wanted to climb on the back and wait for a good meal when the boat had docked. Dad didn't particularly want his life to end that way, so he turned the boat and ran over the animal a couple of times, enough to discourage him from his plans, and the cougar swam back and climbed out of the water.

The point east where the cougar swam out to Dad's boat

There was a family that owned a logging company who purchased the lot on the beach to the west of Esperanza. They were great friends of the mission and became family friends as well. They had four children, and one of them was my age, and we often did things together. Sometimes Mom would invite the family over for dinner, and they would reciprocate. Their home was lovely and modern, and the kids would come over for a visit with the nicest clothes ordered from Sears and Roebuck in the States. We envied their lovely things and their modern ways.

One day, they had an incident with a cougar. The mother was home alone one night when their lovely big dog was attacked. He slept under the house, and the cougar had made his way there to find him. A huge fight ensued. The growls and howls and fighting grew more intense with the animals bumping up against the floorboards as the mother listened helplessly. It went on for quite a while. There was nothing she could do. Finally there was silence. The cougar had won. He dragged that big dog out from under the house and into the woods behind, where his remains were found in the morning.

After a few years, this family pulled their home down the beach and on to a raft so they could tow it to a spot nearer to the new location where their dad was going to log. They towed it down the channel and fastened it securely to the mountainside, still floating on the water. They extended the float so that it housed a bunk house for the men who worked for the company. We often would drive our boat to their home on the water and tie up and have a wonderful visit. The front door opened onto a four-foot walkway that surrounded the home. It was fenced in. If you wanted to go for a swim in the ocean, you just climbed the fence and jumped in. When ships passed by on the channel in front, their home would gently rock as the waves passed under the raft.

I remember going to the bunkhouse on the float with Dad as he handed out Shantyman papers. The loggers were relaxing on their beds as he greeted them, and they had a little chat. There wasn't much in the way of entertainment for the men being locked in by a mountain on one side and the ocean on the other. Dad used every opportunity he had to distribute the gospel to these folks.

By now, the parents of the family are gone, but one sister who lives in Ontario still keeps in contact with some members of our family. I'm not sure where they stood as far as Christianity goes, but she will call, sometimes when she is lonely, sometimes when distressed, sometimes when she's had too much to drink. I find it most intriguing that she will contact the family, from all those decades ago, when life seems a bit too overwhelming. The memory of the mission and the family and what it stood for must be in the back of her mind, with the hope that the message carries and she reaches out for that hope.

We often had experiences with these beautiful but dangerous animals. Cougar hunters were quite often called from town to hunt the animals down. My brother tells of one hunter who came with five dogs, but the cougar managed to kill one of them and injure another. Sometimes we would hear the cougars outside our bedroom windows. Occasionally they would attack small children and often pets that were around. Another time we heard of one that jumped through a window and attacked a man. So we were always on the alert, especially at night.

Tahsis Prince

Stories of the West Coast of Vancouver Island must include boat tales. After all, you can not live in the isolation of the beautiful coastline and not include some intriguing and often frightening sea tales.

Esperanza from the mountain view.

Esperanza is nestled at the base of a hemlock and cedar covered mountain. It is fenced in by a very deep inlet that runs between Nootka Island and Vancouver Island and sharp rugged points to the east and west. The total length of the community is less than half a kilometer from one dock to the other, and even narrower from the barnacled rocky beach where the tide moves in and out several times a day to the base of the forested mountain that acts as our backdrop. It has a southward exposure that soaks up the sun on any days that the typical coastal rains are held in check. Every afternoon, a west wind blows from around nearby Steamer Point and invariably causes whitecaps over the inlet and a cool wind on our shores. Sunny mornings greeted us with a beautiful mirrored sea surface that reflected the mountains of Nootka Island, a mile or two across the channel. The wind was calm in the mornings. This was the view from the living room window of our home that greeted us each sunny day.

The dock to the west was a typical float of timbers built over logs strapped together and held in place by pilings that had been driven into the ground with a pile driver. They were grouped in fours and covered in a black substance to protect the wood from rotting in the water of the salt chuck. The logs floated on the sea and washed up and down whenever waves came towards the beach, passing under the dock. The pilings became home to mussels and barnacles that made for easy bait when we kids took a fancy to go fishing for perch swimming under the dock.

The access to the dock was a ramp that was joined to a strong wooden walkway built high enough to clear any tides. The wooden walkway was also constructed of pilings jammed into the beach and led to a sidewalk going up to the hospital, the center of the small community. The ramp had wheels at the float end to accommodate any changes in tides that brought the float up and down, changing the angle of the ramp. When the tide was low and the water out, the ramp would be at a very steep angle. When the tide was high, especially during a winter storm, the ramp was almost flat.

The tide was always high during storms. Sometimes the water came so far up onto the land that we had to secure the bridge across the larger creek between the hospital and our home, to one of the two huge trees near by. Later a larger bridge was built that was higher and the storms didn't affect it. The ocean often surrounded one of the homes that was on a flat in front of our house during these high tides. Many storms had gales of 100 miles per hour. Sheets of metal flew through the air. Branches too, and as children, we had to hold on to an adult so as not to be blown off our feet. Occasionally, a tied-up seaplane or boat would be sunk or blown over by the wind. The boats certainly were not taken out when a storm was forecast.

This lower dock was "our" dock, built by the mission where the mission boats found their home. It was home to the *Bruce McLean*, the *Lady Carlisle*, the *Mini Bruce*, a small speedboat. In earlier days, there was the *Lizzy*, the *Donna Dean*, and still earlier the *Messenger 11*, the boat that was wrecked at sea with Dad and my brother Bruce on board. (The Messenger 111 came after this boat). This float was also the home to many skiffs and a special canoe built by one of the local Indigenous persons from a neighboring village. He had carved it out of a single large cedar log and sold it to Dad for us three girls. Dottie, my older sister, especially was most enthusiastic about the water and this canoe, and she came up with the name *Doloru Mac* – short for Dorothea, Lois, and Ruth. The native fishing vessels would tie up here as well –sometimes two and three tied to one another, if room was limited.

We enjoyed the tippy canoe and learned to manoeuvre it quite well, one sitting in front steering it with an oar placed at the correct angle in the water, and at other times paddling in sync with the back paddler, which was usually Dottie. And the third one of us enjoying the ride on the middle strip of wood that made a seat. We learned to get in and out without tipping ourselves into the cold ocean by always standing in the middle of the boat with the others helping to balance. Then we would tie it up with a rope to the cleats on the dock or simply around the eight-inch-square timber that edged the dock.

Occasionally, someone would inquire about purchasing the canoe. Of course, we enjoyed it, and selling it was not our intent. One day, it just disappeared, and we found ourselves canoeless. After that, a skiff was what we used to row around the inlet, and the canoe was never found or replaced.

The other dock that was on Esperanza's perimeter was a government-built dock. It was much higher and built to accommodate the ships that were larger and came to provide us with oil, groceries, equipment, and everything needed to live comfortably on the coast.

Barnacle-covered pilings

It too was built by pilings driven into the seabed to secure it against wind, storm, or tide. Again, these pilings were covered in black pitch and became the home to sea urchins and barnacles. There were a couple of small sheds erected on this dock for storage and the housing of gas pumps to fill up the mission boats or those coming to stop from other villages nearby. It was to this dock that the large ocean freighters would come on a regular schedule to deliver our commodities.

There were no shops other than Peterson's store at Esperanza where we bought wagon wheels, as I mentioned earlier. In order to purchase food supplies, individual families or the hospital kitchen staff would need to send an order by mail.

I remember Mom sitting down at the kitchen table after supper dishes were put away and the kitchen back in order. She had a huge Woodward's order sheet and she would look over every column, checking off everything she would need to feed our family for the next month or so. The orders were large and infrequent, so it took some planning. Whole cases of bing cherries, canned beans, peas, tuna fish, pears, peaches, and Campbell's soup were checked off. Cases of Pacific canned milk was our staple and what we grew up on, mixed three-to-one with cold stream water that came through our pipes from the local mountain creek. Roasts, carrots, cabbage, onions, flour, and all the baking needs. Toiletries, brooms, soaps. When she was finished and the order was complete, Mom sealed the envelope and walked over to the tiny little shack that was our post office and with a stamp on the envelope greeted Mrs. Manning the post mistress, as she handed the letter to her for processing.

Two times a week, the mail came in and went out by seaplane. Mrs. Manning stuffed all the mail into large, grey, weathered canvas bags that closed with a strong cord pulled through metal eyes. When the seaplane came to pick up and deliver mail on Tuesdays and Saturdays, Mrs. Manning had her bags all filled and ready to be taken down to the dock by one of the mission men for transfer to the plane. He would stay on the dock talking to the Beaver pilot, helping him load the mail and any passengers that may also be going with him, untie the plane, and watch while it taxied out of reach of the dock, found the wind direction, and revved his engines to take off from the water, with a deafening drone and a huge spray of sea water drifting back to those on the dock. Then he would lift the heavy, incoming, discolored mailbags and walk up the ramp and the walkway to the post office where Mrs. Manning was waiting. She sorted the mail behind closed doors and opened the post office when ready to receive folks anxiously awaiting contact with those on the outside, those in the cities, and friends and family. Or perhaps small parcels from the Eaton's and Simpson Sears catalogues ordered two and three weeks earlier by filling out a form describing the color, size, catalogue number, and price of the article you wanted. Those receiving mail would carry their treasures off to their rooms or home, or maybe go to the hospital lounge to enjoy. Mom's mail was her lifeline. It was her contact with the outside world. She would sit down and write friends and family and look forward to their responses. Each of her letters started with a scripture and then "Greetings in Jesus name" before she began any personal writing. The letters we received from her while we were away at high school in Three Hills had the same greeting and a particularly suitable verse. By the time I was five years old, my brother was a missionary in Japan, and every week he sent Mom a letter so she could keep up with his activities. She would take her airmail letter written on thin blue paper that came from Japan, and every Thursday afternoon invite some mission ladies over for tea and a time of prayer that she called her Japanese prayer meeting, remembering the requests that he had given.

So after Mom had delivered her Woodward's order to the post office, it would be a couple of weeks later that the *Tahsis Prince* would be expected and on it the groceries. The *Tahsis Prince* was one of the main ships that circled the island and delivered goods to each community. It was always exciting when it was time for the boat to come. We usually heard that it was unloading supplies at Tahsis, a town of about 2,000 people and about 20 minutes away by boat, and that it would soon be on its way to us. We waited and watched the point to our east, looking for the bow of the ship or its mast to come into view. Soon we would see it, and the ship would round the point with the wake of the ship ruffling up against the bow as it plowed through the water. The men jumped into the jeep, the only wheels we had on the mission, and drove it from behind the hospital where it was kept by the machine shop, across the wooden bridge over Shirley Creek, passed our house and steps, over the tiny spring that meandered through our yard, through the big cedars and hemlocks, and down the wooden dock in readiness to pick up the ship's cargo and deliver it to our homes. Many of us put on our coats and ran down to the dock to watch as the ship came in and docked, making sure to keep out of the way of flying ropes and unloading of cargo.

The ship was about 200 feet long. It would ease into the dock. The men on board waited for the right time to throw the heavy rope that would anchor it while they were unloading, and our men would catch it and tie the ship securely to the twelve-inch timbers acting also as an edging and sometimes seconded as a seat on the dock's edge. The boat was secured both front and back. Everything was in readiness to begin unloading.

One of the ship's crew members handled the pallet lift by levers directly above the hold of the ship. He could see down into the hold as well as onto the dock and pushed and pulled the right levers to lower the pallet into the hold so that other shippers below could stack boxes and barrels and cargo onto the lift. When the pallet was balanced and sufficiently full, the pallet operator began the motors to lift it out of the hold – up, up, up until it was in view of those of us on the dock – then he pulled another lever, and the pallet began coming towards us, over the ship, over the drop between the ship and the dock, and then easing it slowly down on the wooden planks, making sure it was centered on a spot clear of people, the jeep, and other obstacles. The motor would stop, and then our men got busy unloading the goods off the pallet and sorting them out. Some to go to the McLeans. Some to go to the hospital. Some to go to other families. Larger parcels from Sears or Eaton's would be in a mailbag and delivered to the post office. When the pallet was empty, the operator started up the motor again, and the slack metal ropes holding it would stretch out and begin to lift it up and then back, across the dock, to the boat, and over the hold. Down, down, down the motor would ease it back into the hold for another load. This was repeated until all the shipping for Esperanza was unloaded onto our dock. Farewells were shouted back and forth to the familiar men on board, and the boat's ropes would be loosened and dropped down the side of the ship from where they would be hauled up by a winch by those on board. The captain began the ship's propeller, the water churned up at the stern, and the ship began to move out from the dock and into the channel, on its way to the next stop of Zeballos, another town of about 500 people and about 30 minutes away. We stood on the dock and watched until the ship rounded the point to the west, passing in front of our home and the hospital and our lower mission dock. When the last of its wake was out of sight, we walked back up to the house, waiting on the delivery of our Woodward's groceries ordered by Mom a couple of weeks before.

Ours was the first stop. The jeep stopped on the gravel road by our home, and box after box of groceries was carried through the basement door and placed on the cement floor. Seemed to my young eyes that the basement was full of boxes! It was exciting. Everything from Woodward's was always such good quality. It had that new cardboardy smell. Somehow it smelled like the city to me, mixed with fuel and ocean spray and jeep grease. Now it was Mom's turn to get busy. Before we knew it, the basement floor was covered in a sea of papers and boxes and tins of food of every sort. It was a wonderful feeling of excitement and wonder at the lovely packaging and a larder full of food that would last a good long time. The tins were put neatly away on a shelf, the papers gathered to be taken to the incinerator in front of the hospital. So our groceries were stocked up for another few months. And others on the mission who were expecting deliveries went through a similar process. The boat came every ten days and always the excitement was high. And this was the way our needs were supplied on this little coastal village of Esperanza.

My First Catalogue Order

One day I decided to send in my first order to Simpson Sears. We preferred Simpson Sears to Eaton's for a couple of reasons. It only took two weeks from the time you delivered your order to the post office to receiving it in the mail or by boat. Eaton's took three weeks. Then if the size was wrong, you had to pack it up in the original bags and brown packing paper, go to the post office for stamps, and send it back, which took at least two more weeks, maybe more. You certainly had to begin early in the fall if you wanted to get presents in time for Christmas. And we did order in early October.

The first time I sat down to place an order, I pulled out the order sheet that was tucked away in the back of the catalogue and opened it up to make sure of what it was I wanted. I searched the catalogue pages and began my order by carefully copying down the catalogue number first, then a description of the item, the size, the color number, the price, and taxes. I did the same for the next item and when I was done, I added up the total and made sure my name and address were on the form, put the money – bills, change, and all – into the envelope, and sealed it securely. Off I went, across the bridge, passing in front of the hospital and up the sidewalk to the post office, where I dropped off my letter in the slot for outgoing mail.

It wasn't too long before the phone on our wall by the bathroom rang. One long ring. That was the ring for the McLean house. Two rings was for the hospital. Three rings was for another family. Some had a long and a short. Others two long and one short. But this was for us, and I was called to the phone. It was Mrs. Manning, the post mistress, wondering if I could come over to see her.

Wondering what I had done, I put on my coat and went down the stairs and across the gravel path towards the post office. I unlatched the door and walked up to the opening where Mrs. Manning was in view. It was then she gently explained to me that you don't send money, at least not change for sure, in the mail. I had my first lesson and introduction to the money order and from then on was much wiser in my catalogue ordering, which continued on for many years. And for many years after I had moved to the city, I enjoyed taking the catalogue down from its place on the shelf, leafing through the pages. No more money orders were necessary years later. I simply got the Sears number and called on the phone, and in three or four days, the parcel was in. Much easier on your feet too than shopping the mall. Simpson Sears had long ago been given a shortened name – Sears. Now neither Sears nor Eaton's are in existence. And sending money in the mail? Bills were safe generally then, but certainly not now. The personal touch of a phone call from the local post mistress is also one of years gone by.

The Princess MaQuinna

The *MaQuinna* plied the west side of Vancouver Island in the '40s and '50s before the *Tahsis Prince*, delivering the larger mail parcels not sent up by seaplane and all the freight ordered by folks living on the coast, and was also a beautiful passenger ship. It was our link to the outside world.

My recollections of the *MaQuinna* were of a beautifully built CPR ship with all the quality that implies. It was the means of transportation that we used to go to Vancouver, and because it took several days to get there, staterooms were provided for those going to be on for the duration of the trip.

The ship was boarded by the gangplank let across the water from the ship to the dock. There were the usual things on the ship's deck – white covered lifeboats, huge round white smokestacks, small rounded door entrances that led down into different parts of the ship, a hold that if uncovered revealed all the freight the ship was supplying to the various communities. Ropes, chains, some passenger benches so the fresh air could be enjoyed if the weather permitted and the seas were calm and of course, the bridge where you were not to visit unless by special permission.

Upon descending the stairs to the main floor of the ship, you came into an area that led down two long aisles, one on either side that ran the length of the ship. They were bordered by outside and inside staterooms. Tapestry carpets ran the length of the aisles. They were a lovely rich combination of wine colours in a sort of paisley design. The walls were constructed of warm mahogany. The aisles led to a large oval stairway at the forward of the ship. This was the entrance to the white-linen-draped dining room. The tables were set with heavy silver cutlery and the waiters, all dressed in white with aprons and hats, carried their trays at shoulder level in a most dignified manner and had a white towel draped over their arm. Being little girls, the waiters would often tease us by flicking their towels up the curved stairs where we would be either going or coming. Swinging doors led into the kitchen area, and through portholes high on each side above the tables, you could view the sky from the perspective of the lower dining area. The wonder of the loveliness of the whole ship culminated in the elegance of the dining experience.

The staterooms were furnished in rich, dark, polished mahogany also. Upon entering the room by the solid brass handle of the small but sturdy door and pushing against the control mechanism that kept them from swinging and banging when the seas got rough, you encountered a step over sill that led into the room. The built in bunk was directly in front of you. There was a sense of spaciousness in the room. To the left and against the outer wall was a built-in bench seat with a full-length cushion that fit nicely with the warm, polished wood and the wine-patterned carpet. Directly above the seat was a porthole with sturdy brass closures that could be opened for fresh air and closed when the ship began to roll. In between the bed and the bench seat was a small white sink with taps and sturdy round handles and always a couple of individual paper-covered CPR soaps. It was enclosed in the same wood, and a mirror above completed the room. Bathrooms were down the aisle, clean and white, the floor tiled in tiny black and white squares and again with a step over sill at the entrance. Every detail was awe-inspiring for us as children, the quality of which I don't think you can find today. There were sitting areas and lounges scattered here and there, and always the whole ship was a vision of quality and loveliness.

I remember Mom made us sit on the built-in bench in our room and practice our duets and trios as the ship continued on its journey. On one of these trips, we were just four and five and on our way to Ontario to visit uncles and aunts on my dad's side of the family. It was in Ontario that we sang in several churches and over a radio station, and for many years after, we sang duets and trios.

Sometimes we didn't like singing or practising, and one time, at the end of our song in a large church, my younger sister ran over to Mom, who was playing the piano, and said, loud enough for the congregation to hear, "Do we have to sing anymore?" A ripple of chuckles spread across the church.

The Messenger III

The *Messenger III* was a sturdy-built sea-worthy boat of about 50 feet and was operated by the Shantymen. The Shantymen were missionaries that visited and looked after the spiritual needs of those folks who lived in isolated areas. Their name originated many years ago when missionaries spent their time visiting folks who lived in shanties far off and away from largely populated areas. One of their policies was not to be stationed on property but to travel. The West Coast was an ideal area for the Shantymen to operate a boat that circled the island and visited the different Indigenous villages, logging camps, fishing floats, lighthouses, and secluded spots where single families or individuals chose to live. One such spot was a little cove across from Esperanza called God's Pocket. It was a small, protected bay where a couple known as the Rustands lived for years. They came over to Esperanza occasionally when the weather was nice, in their little 12-foot aluminum boat that sported a small outboard engine. They would putt-putt along to the dock, tie up the boat, and come to the mission for a visit or supplies or mail.

One Christmas, when we schoolchildren had just finished our concert with all the parents proudly in attendance and were dressed in our Christmas best, Mr. Rustand came down the stairs of the Esperanza hotel, where we had the event in the large dining room that had been turned into a small auditorium for the evening, and he played the role of Santa Claus, giving out brown bags of candy and oranges and candy canes for each one of us. He had finished his Santa act and left the room to return upstairs to change out of his suit when he took a heart attack and died. It was a shock to us all.

Mrs. Rustand lived alone in God's Pocket for many years after the death of her husband.

The *Messenger* would stop in for a visit to the mission whenever they were in the area, and we looked forward to their visits with much anticipation. It was wonderful to see the ship quietly glide into the dock and to watch as Uncle Harold Peters, the skipper, manoeuvre it into place. Then out he came from the wheelhouse, hands in the air and a smile on his face, greeting us in his soft, mellow voice – his greeting always warm and chuckly – sporting his heavy tweed pants that kept him warm in the cool breezes of the Pacific. Uncle Percy Wills was often along on these trips around the island.

From the left are Percy Wills, Dad, and Harold Peters, the skipper of the Messenger

It was Uncle Percy who first introduced Dad to the West Coast in 1937. He had heard that there was a young doctor at Prairie Bible Institute and wrote him a letter introducing himself and inviting Dad to come to the coast to view the medical needs of the locals there. Dad and Mom had planned to go to Africa as missionaries, under the mission where Phil Keller's parents were supervising.

Phil Keller was a friend of the family and the Shantymen and authored many books, one being about the Shantymen on the coast entitled *Splendor From the Sea*. He was a wonderful godly man. We were privileged to know him and be on his sheep farm in Sooke, B.C. From his farming experience, he wrote another book called *A Shepherd Looks at the 23rd Psalm*, with great insight into the life of sheep and how it relates to our lives as Christians. Many church libraries have this insightful book.

My parents were preparing to be missionaries in Africa. Mom was happy to go to Africa, but the West Coast of Vancouver Island? "No thanks," she let Dad know in no uncertain terms. However, Mom was turned down medically for Africa due to the condition of her feet, which the doctors deemed unsuitable for traversing the trails in the deeps of the continent.

Dad went from Three Hills, where he had received the invitation from Percy Wills, to the West Coast to view the medical and spiritual needs there. The two men got into a boat and began a tour of the west side of the island. There were loggers, fishermen, Indigenous villages, coastal people, and several large communities, all within several hundred miles with no medical hospital. It would take hours or days to get help in case of illness or accident. Dad saw the need, and after much prayer and consideration and discussion with Mom, it was decided that this is where the Lord was directing them.

Percy Wills was a close associate of our family. It was wonderful to see him too when the *Messenger* came for a visit. Usually the stay was a day or two. The crew would bring up their laundry, and I remember several times the ironing board out in the middle of our kitchen while one of the folks ironed and chatted with Mom. Often, as children, we sat on the knees of Uncle Percy or Uncle Harold. We would gather together for a special meeting and enjoy the wonderful blending of voices of these men as they treated us to some old favorites in duet.

Sometimes, several of the staff would get on board the *Messenger* and go for a trip somewhere. As kids, we scooted around the ship, up to sit on the bow and enjoy the breezes and view as Uncle Harold guided us safely along. Or we walked down the sides, holding the wire railing to go to the galley, which opened onto the back landing of the boat where you could also sit if the breezes were too stiff up front.

The galley had a typical narrow ship entrance and three steps down from the back. On the left was the small ship stove, complete with a metal rail to keep pots in place if the ship rolled. Beside the stove was a small counter and sink where delicious meals were prepared by whomever was cooking. The galley had bunks on each side that doubled as seating during the day and, of course, a table. Lighting was provided by portholes up high above the bunks, and there were the odd racks around to keep magazines and odds and ends. Cupboards with latched doors lined the bottom of the portholes. When the ship entered rough water, the dishes in the cupboards rolled and rattled.

Directly across from the entrance to the galley, at the midpoint of the boat, was a low door into the engine room. The engine sat on the floor right in the middle of the room and always smelled of diesel. You had to walk around it to make your way to the tiny bathroom equipped with a ship toilet. Off this engine room was a step over sill to the bow-shaped bedroom with a built-in double bunk and drawers underneath. Although we had many trips on the *Messenger*, there was one time we were privileged to sleep here in this forward bunk. The boat was going to leave early in the morning, so this way we were there and ready to go. We woke up to the engine warming up and the boat pulling away from the dock. We were on our way. There was a ladder up from here into the wheelhouse, Uncle Harold's main stay. The wheelhouse had the usual large ship's wheel and another bunk at the rear under some sunny windows that looked out towards the top of the galley and to the aft of the ship. Many times, we would gather in the wheelhouse and join in singing with Uncle Harold as he guided the ship along, some sitting on the box that covered the ladder entrance to the bedroom below, some sitting on Uncle Harold's bunk bed, others standing in the doorway and around the wheelhouse.

Well, the time was always too short, and the crew would get ready to depart. Many of the staff came to the dock to say their goodbyes and watch as they prepared to go. When everything was loaded, Uncle Harold warmed up the ship's engine and the deckhands (usually some young Bible school students who had come along for experience) untied the bow and stern, and after hugs and waves, the boat slowly moved away from the dock. As we stood on the dock, we sang together:

Blest be the tie that binds
Our hearts in Christian love
The fellowship of kindred minds
Is that of Christ above.

Or

Till we mee-ee-eet, till we mee-eet
Till we meet, at Jesus feet,
Till we mee-ee-eet, till we mee-eet,
God be with you till we meet again.

They were on the ship, standing out back, waving, and we on the dock singing and waving, many times with tears, always sad to see them go, and we watched until the ship had rounded the point and was out of sight. Then we made our way up the ramp and the walkway back to our post on the mission, whether in the hospital kitchen or the nursing area or to our homes, and life continued on our little patch of land by the sea.

Hungerford's Anniversary

Mr. Hungerford was a middle-aged single man who lived on a cleared piece of land just before you rounded the point on the last lap of the journey to Tahsis. It was about 10 to 15 minutes from the mission. He was not part of the Esperanza staff but came often to visit.

One day, Mr. Hungerford decided to take aim at a crow sitting on a telephone pole that was out in front of the hospital. He fired his gun and missed.

My brother Garth was around eight years old, and he was visiting with friends in a nearby building at the time. Garth was sitting in front of the window, chatting, when all of a sudden, he grabbed the back of his head and doubled over in pain. No one was quite sure what had happened.

The shot that had missed the crow had ricocheted off the telephone post and gone through the window and hit Garth directly in the back of the head. Dad was away at Tahsis when this happened so the staff called him on the radio phone. It took him an hour or so to close up his office and go down to the dock to make the journey back to Esperanza. When he arrived Dad took him into the operating room when it was discovered what had happened and put Garth to sleep to extract the bullet. It was embedded deeply, just touching his brain. Carefully, Dad removed it, wondering what effect this was going to have on his son.

It was decided that Garth needed to be sent to Vancouver to see a specialist, so Mom boarded the *MaQuinna*, leaving her baby in the care of the nurses in the hospital and her other children in good hands, and took Garth to Vancouver. His vision was gone. No one knew what the outcome of this accident would be.

The doctors in Vancouver did further surgery and discussed whether a metal plate should be placed in Garth's skull. After a time of recovery, his sight returned, and they returned home. The family was thankful that he was alright and his vision had returned.

Many years later, Mr. Hungerford married a staff member, Edith, who joined him at his home on his little isolated spot by the sea. It was on their anniversary one year that we decided to pay this couple a surprise visit on this special occasion.

The summer evening was sunny and warm as our family went down to the wharf to get into the *Bruce*. This kind of family outing happened very seldom, unless it was a scheduled summer holiday when plans were made to go to the city. Mostly we did things together as a staff group, so it was with pleasure that Dad started the engine while my sister and I untied the front and back ropes and put the tires that served to protect the boat from rubbing against the dock, back onto the roof by the skiff. Every boat had a skiff in case of emergency. We pushed the boat out away from the wharf so Dad could back out safely and jumped on. Holding the rail on top, we edged our way down the side and into the cab of the boat. When we were back down and inside, Dad put the boat in full gear and with the bow up and a good wake at the back, we sped towards the Hungerford's home.

We pulled up to their float dock and after securing the boat for the evening, we walked up the wooden walkway that led to their home. They were surprised to see us and welcomed us warmly to their comfortable little home. We sat around the table looking out onto the bay and our boat docked below and were warmed by the kitchen stove where Edith had made tea. After an evening of pleasant chatting, it was dark and time to go home, so we said goodbye and made our way back down to the dock.

We were well on our way in the damp, dark of an ocean evening. I was tired so I laid down on the bench seat behind Mom. There were two front seats, one on the right where Mom sat chatting with Dad and watching the water for debris and one on the left where Dad operated the boat. I always sensed that I should be up there too, helping Dad watch for deadheads or logs. If the night was especially dark, he would have one hand on the handle on the roof that operated the spotlight outside and the other on the steering wheel. He manoeuvred the light back and forth over the water, making sure there was nothing of danger. But I was tired and, even though my conscience told me I should be helping – and Dad was probably as tired as I was – I continued to lie there, with the motor just a couple of feet away, warming me up.

Dad began to steer the boat rather erratically. The boat went left for a bit and then right and then back towards the left, and I wondered what was happening. All of a sudden, he slowed it right down and with the gearshift on the floor, put the boat in reverse just before there was a loud bang and the boat lurched to a stop. "Dad's run into the mountain," I thought and jumped up to look out the window. Dad was opening his side window, explaining that a boat had run into us. A couple of intoxicated men in a speedboat were on their way from Zeballos to Tahsis, and when they saw the light of our boat, they kept coming towards the light. As Dad turned left to get away from them, they would come toward us. So back he would go to the right and finally he decided if they were going to hit us it would be better if our boat were going in reverse to reduce the force of the impact. It would also lower the bow, which was always at a good height at top speed. He no sooner got into reverse than they came up on our bow before their engine died and the boat dropped back down into the water. They took quite a chunk out of the bow of the boat, but it was high enough not to puncture the hull and sink us.

All was silent. The men were stunned and in shock. Dad hollered out the window across the dark water to them. They were at a distance from our boat now, drifting in the channel, so Dad asked them if they were alright. We could just barely see across the dark water. There was some mumbling, and it was apparent they had been drinking.

Dad put the boat in gear and slowly moved towards them. One of the men had a severe gash in the corner of his eye from the windshield breaking, and Dad could see he needed some medical attention. He got their rope and tied the speedboat up to the back of the *Bruce* after taking the injured man on board with us. The other man wanted to stay in his boat, so he came along behind. After we started on our way again with the boat in tow, the man in the speedboat behind us started his engine and we wondered if we would be rammed from the back now!

With our boat smelling of liquor while the injured man sat bleeding where I had been lying, we made our way to Esperanza. Dad took the men to the hospital and stitched up the injury the one had received.

Many months later, I remember the police coming to our home with their report. It had been decided that the accident was 50-50. Dad just winked a knowing wink at us and let the matter drop. He never justified himself but felt the Lord would take care of him which He always did. I have always remembered that and felt admiration for Dad's stance in that regard.

Day Trips to Ferrier Point

Each spring, as the warm sun took the chill off the damp coastal air and with the likelihood that the waters would be calm, the folks at the mission would make an annual picnic trip to Ferrier Point, our campground out on the Pacific, on a remote corner of Nootka Island.

The timing of our trip was determined by the tide. It had to be high in order to avoid rocks and reefs on the way to camp, and it was always at some unearthly early morning hour so that everyone was up with the birds. Down to the wharf we went with our lunches packed, a warm coat, gum boots, and all the necessary gear for an outing to Ferrier. Climbing on board, we were soon on our way west, around Steamer Point and out towards the open and Centre Island. There were a couple of Indigenous villages out that way. Queens Cove, where I had gone with Dad when he played the song by George Beverly Shea and Nuchatlitz. If the tide was high, we could go on the inside passage through the very rugged rocks by Nuchatlitz, winding our way carefully. It cut down on time and rough water. But if the tide wasn't at the right level, we would go on the outside passage where the boat would rock considerably, and usually we were a little tense. On one of these occasions, Dad drove the boat on the inside route, but the tide was by now not at optimal height. My sister lay out on the bow of the boat watching for rocks to warn Dad. On another of these trips, the waves were much higher than our boat. We were down in a trough with huge rollers on each side. Usually Dad steered the boat directly into the rollers but for some reason we found ourselves down in the trough. I was nervous. Standing out at the back of the boat, looking up at the waves above me, suddenly over the top of the roller came a small skiff with a sail that was manned by two local Indigenous villagers, sailing calmly over the sea! And there was I in a much larger boat and scared! I guess they made it safely to shore! I never heard otherwise.

Another time on one of these trips back from Ferrier, Earl Johnson was driving the boat. Earl and his wife Louise had taken over the mission after Dad retired and the hospital had closed, and he was a good friend of the family. This day he was manning our speedboat, and we were going unusually fast, at least I thought, for the condition of the sea. But Earl had his seaman's license, so I knew he must know what he was doing. We sat out at the back with the wind blowing our hair and spray from the ocean dampening our faces. We were bouncing and banging over the waves coming back from the camp so that we couldn't keep on our seats. He was bouncing us right off them. Dad's boat was bigger and drove differently in the waves, but this little aluminum boat just bounced and banged from wave top to wave top, and it didn't seem to bother Earl a bit. I guess, after all, the matter of import was not whether we were sitting on our seats or on the floorboards but that we got out of the rough water as quickly as possible and into the sheltered sea!

Lois in one of the smaller speedboats

So we would get to Ferrier about an hour and a half after leaving the mission. Rounding the point at the end of our journey put us into a protected bay and away from the rough sea. Before us was a large expanse of sandy shallow beach. Finding a good place to anchor, the men would go out back and rattle the chain preparing to lift the heavy steel over the side and lower it carefully into the water and to the bottom until it grabbed securely onto some solid object. The lifeboat was lowered from the roof over the back and eased into the sea alongside the boat, and we were ready to transfer into the tippy skiff for transport ashore. When a load was safely in the skiff and the oars in place in the oarlocks, off they rowed towards the beach. The dip of the oar into the still water would leave a neat expanding ripple. Sometimes the oars would bring up long green strands of seaweed or bottom-of-the-ocean grasses that dripped and swayed with the motion of the oar. Back into the water, the oar sliced in a mesmerizing rhythm.

Being a shallow bay, you could row only so far until the bottom of the skiff touched the sand, so some of us rolled up our jeans, removed our shoes and socks, and stepped carefully over the side into the warm bay water. We pulled the skiff up a ways on the sandy beach, so a few didn't have to get their feet wet. When the first load was on shore, the rower would go back for the rest until we were all on the beach with our lunches and jackets.

The beautiful beaches at Ferrier

We headed up the trail to the campsite. It had been built as a lookout during the war, complete with bunkhouses, cookhouse, outdoor bathrooms built over a large cement holding tank, and trails here and there leading to cabins in different parts of the site, some down in among large fir, cedar, and hemlock trees and overlooking the ocean. The cabins were rough. They were now, after many years, housing rusted metal bunk beds with springs, maybe eight or ten sets to a cabin. In preparation for a summer camp some staff members would take a barge full of all the things needed for a camp and that included mattresses for our beds. The girls always had this very rough cabin looking cozy and inviting by the time we had our colorful quilts on them, our clothing hung on nails, and a few items on bedside tables. At night, we heard mice running everywhere and occasionally we would hear a hungry cougar crying outside our walls.

The trees around the campsite had sticks nailed to them to form ladders to the top so the ocean could be viewed more accurately – a leftover lookout from the war. Another very long trail led to the lookout tower. It was about two miles in length and would be an annual camping excursion that took the greater part of a day. The trails had originally been built of sturdy wooden planks suitable for jeeps to drive up out of the mud and uneven ground. But as the years went by, little by little they began to deteriorate until today there is barely any sign of the structure. There was a wonderful beach cutoff on the way to the tower, which we sometimes detoured to. There was another beach behind the cookhouse, which took you deep into the woods, down some steep mossy embankments, and out onto a very rugged shoreline where the breakers would come in and out. Very picturesque and one of my favorite beaches. We would sit up on the high rocks and watch the rollers break on the beach, or stand at the water's edge and run to beat the high waves that would crash in around your feet. There were lots of shells to collect and sea animals of all sorts. Land animals too, like cougar, bear, and raccoon. Every evening during camp, the leaders would build a bonfire on the beach and have a singsong around it. One night we slept down there, right out in the open, and roasted bread over the fire and slathered it with jam. A few brave souls went skinny-dipping. We managed to keep out of the incoming tide and awoke to a dew-covered sleeping bag with the accompanying dampness.

After the day was done on this annual day trip and we had gone on all the expeditions that we had time and energy for, we headed back to the beach for our return home. Of course, we kept an eye out for any sign of weather changes that might cause a dangerous sea. And then there was the consideration of the tides to be mindful of. On the beach, we repeated our skiff trips back and forth to the boat until all were on the *Bruce* again. The anchor was brought up out of the water, sea grass coming along. The men lifted the skiff back up on top of the boat and secured it with ropes, and we turned around and headed back out around the point and into the rough sea, returning back home after a tiring, windswept day at camp.

It was on one of these spring day trips that I instead had gone to a small village called Muchalet, which was near the spot where Gold River now stands. I was maybe 10 or 11 years of age.

There was a couple living in Muchalet called the Maloneys, and I was spending a few days with them. Mrs. Maloney worked during the day, so when I woke up, the house was empty, the table set with a fresh loaf of white Sunbeam bread, a cut of butter, and a Sunbeam pop-up toaster. Our bread at home came in a huge box from the baker at Zeballos, brown and white and unsliced for the whole mission compound. Dad would bring it back on one of his Monday or Thursday weekly trips for the mission and hospital. So I enjoyed piece after piece of this wonderful toasted "city" bread and real butter and the magic of a shiny pop-up toaster! Put a piece in the toaster, watch it pop up, smother it with butter, and enjoy! How wonderful it tasted! There was never a mention of the disappearing loaf, but I have wondered if they were a little surprised at the amount I enjoyed each morning.

When it was time for me to come home, the seaplane flew into the dock, and I climbed on board with a few other passengers. The inside of this one was arranged differently than most of the planes we travelled in. The seats lined the sides with quite a lot of leg space down the middle. Most other planes had two seats across and several rows, depending on the size of the plane (making it far more conducive to grabbing the man in front if you encountered an air pocket!).

We were flying along over the mountains and down the channels when the pilot cut the engine, allowing us to coast for a time. For someone already nervous to be in the air, this was a little unsettling to say the least. However, he restarted the engine, and in a few minutes, we were taxiing into the Esperanza dock.

As I walked up the dock, the mission seemed unusually quiet. It seemed that all but a skeleton staff had gone on their day trip to Ferrier Point. Our house was empty. No one was walking around the grounds. The machine shop was quiet except for the generator back in the trees that kept the mission in power. It was strange.

So with our dog Spottie with me, I decided to climb up the hill behind the hospital where our little one-room school was situated, as well as another building called the dorm. A young mission couple lived there and had not gone on the boat trip, so I decided to go for a visit. But at the bottom of the hill, Spottie simply refused to go past the small platform in the bushes that had a couple of oil barrels standing on it. I coaxed and coaxed, and he looked anxious. Finally, with enough persuasion, he came along past the barrels and platform, and up the hill we climbed to knock on the back door. It was woodsy and there was always the danger of cougars, but we didn't usually worry about it during the daylight hours.

So we visited for a while, and when it was about supper time and time to go home, I said goodbye, but Spottie simply wouldn't come along. So I left him there on their back porch and came down the hill by myself, thinking not too much about it. He would come home later, we were sure.

But he stayed on their porch all evening, and no amount of scolding would change his mind. Then as it got dark, he began to scratch on the door wanting to come in. The couple only opened it up and told him to go home, leaving him there on the porch. After a couple more episodes of this, they went to bed with our little brown and white dog, with his tail curled up over his backside, at their back door, begging to come in and frantically scratching the door.

Well, we never saw Spottie again. Apparently, a cougar had been hiding under the platform that was at the bottom of the hill as we passed by, and he crept up the hill after our pet during the dark of night. And Spottie instinctively knew it and was begging for protection from the cougar that was slinking through the bushes with the thought of a good meal at hand. This was the ending of many of our pets out there in the wilderness.

Dad

This morning I read Dr. Charles Stanley's devotional, and it reminded me of my dad.

> "Regardless of what you are facing, remember these three truths:
> The Lord Jesus Christ stands with you; He strengthens you for whatever you must endure or undertake; and He will enable you to fulfill His purpose until your last dying breath."

As I think of Dad and his years at home on the West Coast, many pictures come to mind. He was not a man to express his feelings too readily, at least in words. You could see them in his expression. We knew he loved us, but I don't remember it being said. He showed it by his actions, and we never wondered about the possibility that he didn't.

Dad was of the stock that felt self-denial was essential to following God. Many fellow students at Prairie High School in Alberta also experienced the same thinking by their parents in those years. Therefore, many missionary kids were sent to the school for their education and felt the separation keenly. Some with detrimental effects, at least temporarily. However, in most cases, once the kids became adults and recovered from resentment, their difficulties turned into character strengtheners and enabled them to become useful servants of the same God their parents served. These days, the thinking has changed that God has given children to parents to care for and nurture and should come first rather than be sacrificed by separation. We were well looked after when we were away from home and had the privilege of staying home at least until high school. I know of some missionary children who left home in their elementary years if no school was available on their mission. I'm not sure personally which belief is correct. The Lord certainly blessed Mom and Dad for their sacrifice, and their children all rose up and called them blessed.

Our dad practised this same ideology, although the sacrifice was more on his part than on ours. He wouldn't give in to his own desire to spend time at home because that would not be giving himself completely to God, he felt. My brothers felt this lack of time spent with their dad most keenly, so they joined him in clearing trees, building houses, and going on boat trips to wherever it was Dad was headed. Dad never took time for things like fishing, even though the ocean was right there. And he wouldn't allow a gun in the house, so hunting was out of the question. The mission to him entailed medicine and spreading the gospel. But I think it was Mom who took the greatest brunt of this. We remember her many days in the bedroom crying. She was lonely for Dad. Even though he was home for each meal, his days and evenings were spent at the hospital. If she wanted to be with him, she needed to join him on one of his four-day-a-week outings to Tahsis or Zeballos. So that is what she did.

Mom made arrangements for Miss Covey, a sweet, little, grey haired, single staff member, to come to the house and manage we three girls on Tuesdays. She would spend the afternoons with the wall ironing board down, sprinkling the washed and line-dried clothes, rolling them up to dampen, and then ironing all afternoon standing there by the window. Dad wore white shirts every day, so there was always plenty to iron. White handkerchiefs, shirts, tablecloths, pillowcases, blouses, our little pink plaid Sunday skirts all needed ironing. Then she would make supper for us. We usually requested canned corn and tuna fish. Sometimes, my older sister would play mean tricks on this very proper little lady who never had any of her own kids, especially the likes of these who played sometimes not-so-pleasant tricks on her! And then when it was bedtime, Miss Covey would take her hot iron and open our beds and iron the sheets warm before we jumped in. After pulling our blinds, which faced the woods at the back of the house, she'd quietly sit on the edge of our bed and sing in her shaky little voice, "Now the day is over, night is drawing nigh. Shadows of the evening creep across the sky," and we would be spooked to sleep!

Meanwhile, Mom had gone down to the dock to board our boat, the *Bruce*, with Dad and off they went to Tahsis. Dad would find his motorcycle and go off to open his medical office for the town folk, and Mom would visit at some of the homes, or other times she held a Bible study. Sometimes, Dad would bring back Wrigley's Juicy Fruit gum for us or a brick of ice cream that he purchased at the Tahsis Co-op, both of which were real treats for us. He would keep the ice cream as cold as possible by setting it on the floorboards out at the back of the boat until he arrived back at Esperanza. Then it was sliced into five and eaten quickly before it melted. Fridges didn't come to our home until the later 1950s, so we had no way to keep frozen foods.

Mom and Dad took turns waking us up in the mornings for school. When it was Dad's turn, he often came into our room and did a little tap dancing. It didn't last long as he was soon out of breath. But after we were dressed and our beds made, we would come to the kitchen table and wait as Dad stirred the porridge on the stove. When breakfast was done and the table cleared, we then went to the front room to sing while Mom played the piano. Occasionally, if Mom was away, Dad would play, but his playing was somewhat like his typing – the two-finger variety. After a few songs, we read the Bible and then all knelt down to pray around the circle. And then we as children were off to school. Dad would do up the breakfast dishes before he walked over to the hospital for the day's work.

Dad had already been up early and off to the hospital at 6 am each morning to have devotions and prayer with the staff. This is the way the day began for the mission folk. They met in the lower dining room and all got down on their knees to pray after a reading of scripture before they went off to their different locations to work.

Years later I heard a lady speak of her childhood years at Esperanza, and one day, she walked past the walkway above the dining room and, as she peered in the window, she stopped and watched this scene, all the staff on their knees in the dining room. It had affected her greatly and now that she was a mother with her own children, she wished they too could have that wonderful opportunity, to see folks on their knees before the Lord.

After our morning routine was complete, we left our home to walk to the school that was behind the hospital and up the hill. We were also able to come for lunch. Dad would again join us. Usually, Mom warmed up Campbell's soup or leftover macaroni and cheese, opened a can of peaches, and always a plate of bread and butter was served at each meal. When we excused ourselves from the table, we stood before Mom to say our memory verse in preparation for the coming Sunday and then made our way again to school for the afternoon session. The kids who had come to school from surrounding villages in the school boat had their lunches with them and stayed in the school. We often envied them having lunches in lunch kits.

The school looked out across the channel to Nootka Island where Hecate was located. It was a small grouping of dorms and homes and was operated by Esperanza. We used to have our annual conferences there. It was originally a reduction plant built up on pilings out over the water but had long since been abandoned. Some of our staff members lived at Hecate as well as a few Indigenous families. They would come back and forth in little boats to Esperanza for get-togethers and Sunday services and Wednesday evening prayer meetings, which were held in the lounge of the hospital so patients and staff and mission workers alike could attend.

On Wednesdays, I would go to the dock with the school kids and join them in the school boat on their way home to Hecate for my weekly piano lesson, join the family for dinner, and come back with them for the evening service. I remember having porcupine meatballs there for the first time and thought it was neat how the rice poked out of the meatballs like porcupine quills. The school boat made the rounds every morning to pick up kids from the surrounding spots of Hecate and CeePeeCee, which was just around the point from us and about a five-minute drive away. The boat would bring them back to Esperanza with their lunch kits for a day at school. Then at the end of the day, the kids would gather on the dock to board the little speedboat again and return home.

The hospital

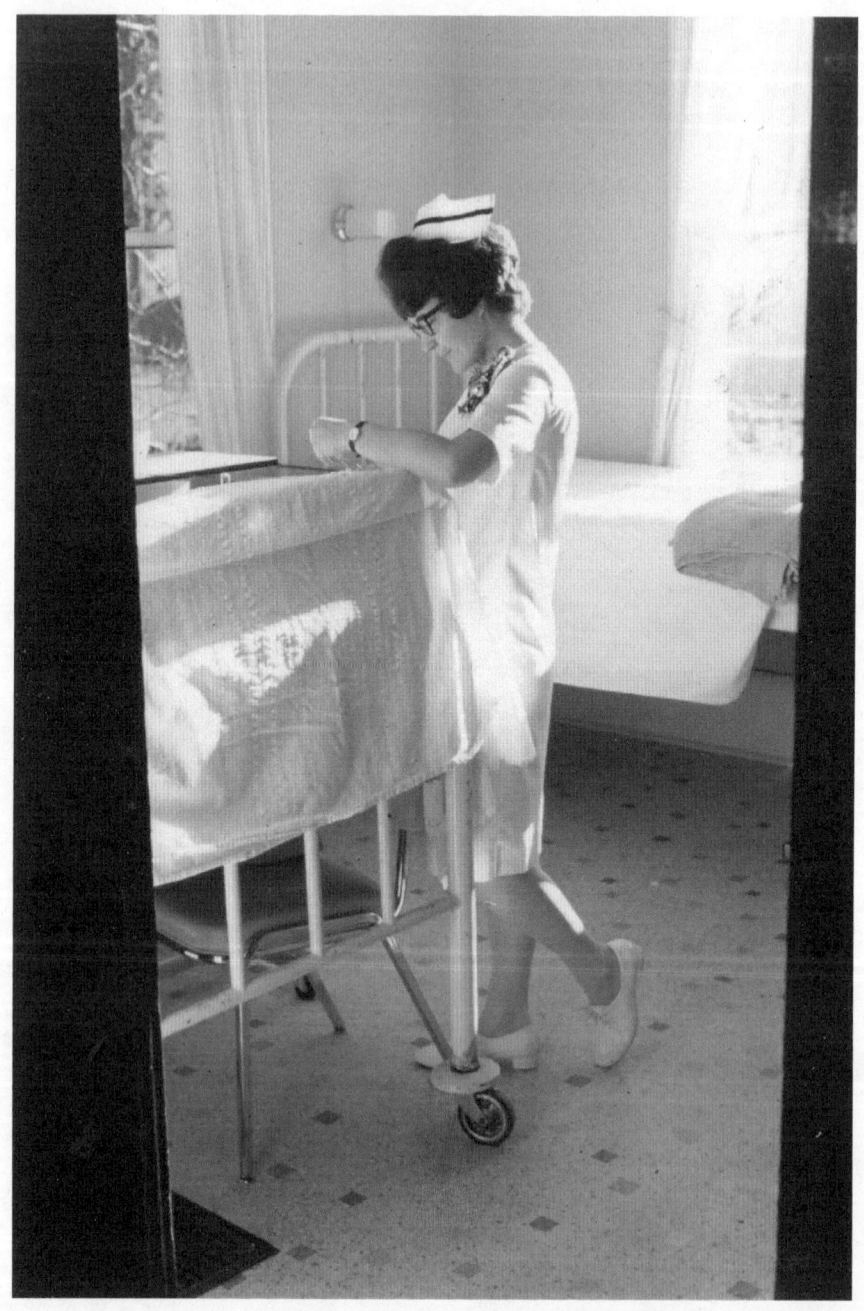

A nurse in the hospital room facing our home

Dad would share experiences of the day as we sat together around the kitchen table. One I especially remember was a logging accident patient who arrived from the local village of Chamiss Bay. He didn't share medical situations often, but this one he did. The logger had been up on the mountain with a partner when the tree they were falling dropped right across his lower body. His partner had to climb over the mountain to get help and return with a stretcher and manpower to load him up and then again scale the mountain to the dock where a plane had been advised of the accident. He was flown to Esperanza for medical help. His situation was dire, and as Dad told the story, his eyes filled with tears at the memory of the excruciating pain the man was in.

Occasionally, while we were sharing dinner together, someone rapped at the door. It was generally a staff member who'd come for a visit. Dad would pull up a chair, and the adults had a visit right there around the table. Dad's eyes would glint with joy as he chatted happily with the visitor, sharing jokes or comical situations. He loved company and felt right at home with them. Mom was more formal although always gracious, but Dad would move his chair back and have a good chat. If the conversation became a little risqué, Mom would say, "Oh Herman!" with her cheeks aflush, and Dad would chuckle but mind her dislike for the topic of conversation.

And again Dad would excuse himself from the dinner table and be off to the hospital for book work or patient care. And Mom was alone for the evening. The days he had gone to one of the local villages for regular office openings, he would not be with us around the table. We watched out our kitchen window by the table and saw the light of his boat drive by on the channel in front of our home. He was coming home in the dark, and we were relieved once again that Dad was safely home. The ocean at night could be a challenge with storms, pelting rain, or fog that made the trip dangerous.

The demands of the hospital kept Dad busy. Occasionally, he had help when another physician would come to the mission. But generally he carried the load and loved his work. Many times he would be up at night to emergencies but always back at the hospital for his daytime duties. If he was tired, he would never go to bed during the day but would stretch out on the couch with his shoes carefully over the end so as not to soil it. And he would go to sleep. As a little girl, I watched his heart beating so that it shook his body and it scared me. Dad had an enlarged heart due to overwork. He used to carry patients up the stairs to the operating room until his heart wouldn't take it. It was also discovered in his last months in the hospital at the end of his life that he had a hole in his heart, which would also have added to the condition. I wondered as a girl what we would do if Dad died. Mom could never understand why he wouldn't just go to bed in the bedroom, but he liked being right there in the middle of his family and the activities.

One of the nurses tells a story of when she first came to the mission from her nurses' training in Ontario. What a difference between the huge hospital there and the small 26-bed one on the coast, if you included the children's ward! She worked in an operating room in Ontario and told of the doctors at times in anger throwing instruments across the room in the middle of surgery. But her first morning in the OR at Esperanza, Dad was operating on a little boy about 18 months old, and he knew there was nothing more he could do for the child. So he held the little boy up in his arms and said, "Lord, there is nothing more I can do for this boy. Will you help him?" And the new nurse was amazed at this holy dedication and completely different perspective.

A little girl about eight years of age came in for surgery one day. She was so afraid that when the nurses brought her in to the operating room and helped her up on the OR table, she cried uncontrollably. They tried to calm her, but nothing seemed to be helping. So finally the nurse asked her if she knew any songs she could sing. The little girl started singing "Jesus Loves Me," and the nurses and Dad sang right along with her. After a few more choruses, the little girl looked at Dad and smiled, and they knew they could put her to sleep and proceed with the surgery.

Dad always prayed with the patient and the surgical staff before he administered anesthetic. And occasionally, when an emergency arose in the operating room, a plea for prayer was sent out to the mission staff. Mom also received these messages and got down on her knees by her bed to pray. Many times, hemorrhages and other medical emergencies were stopped by prayer.

Saturday mornings, Mom and Dad would enjoy a quiet breakfast together before we girls got out of bed. After the meal was over, they would read the Bible and get on their knees to pray. We would hear them praying from our bedroom for each member of the family, starting with Max the oldest, down to Don, then Shirl, Garth (Bruce was already gone in a shipwreck), Dot,

Lois, and Ruth. Other Saturdays, Dad would fix a nice tray for Mom. His tray generally included a soft-boiled egg, toast, and coffee, complete with salt and pepper and jam, and he would carry it into the bedroom as a special treat for Mom. She would be studying her Bible, perched up in bed. There were no shops or malls, so this was a little outing of sorts for Mom.

Prayer was a big part of Mom and Dad's life on the coast. Occasionally, I would see Dad kneeling by his bed with the covers turned back, just before he climbed in. Always kneeling. Their prayers got them through the rugged times on the coast, and God answered many urgent prayers offered to Him.

When we were very ill, Dad put us in the hospital. I remember when the Asiatic flu came around; it was in the spring just before our conference time. I was all prepared for this special occasion when folks from the city came, we had special speakers, and often the *Messenger 111* came to be with us with the wonderful Shantyman missionaries. I remember sitting on the couch and not even realizing I was coming down with something. It turned out to be the Asiatic flu. Dad took me to the hospital, and I was there for a long time. The nurses gave me alcohol baths to try to get my fever down. It was so high, my throat would bleed. I seemed to be semi-conscious, and Dad had asked Miss Parry, the hospital cook, to sit by my bed because even at that age, I tended towards delirious episodes when my fever was high. I don't know who was taking her place in the kitchen. Through my foggy mind, I heard Dad come down the hall of the hospital singing "Heavenly Sunshine". His favorite verse was Romans 8:28: "And we know that all things work together for good for those who love God and are called according to His purpose." Then one day, he entered my sick room and stated that he might have to fly me out to Vancouver because they were unable to get my fever down. I was afraid of the seaplanes that we had to take to leave Esperanza for town and I don't know if that scared the fever out of me, but I soon got well.

The rooms of the hospital were lovely with their view of the ocean. The one I was in when I was ill this time was facing our home across the bridge, and I could see Mom walking around the house doing her housework from my hospital room when I was well enough to get out of bed. I was in this same room one day as a very small child when I had put my arm in the wringer washing machine. It must have been Monday as that was Mom's wash day, and she had gone upstairs for something. I was maybe three or four, and the wringer part of the washing machine intrigued me. I picked up a sock and began feeding it into the rollers that squeezed out the water, and my fingers went in with the sock. I must have hollered as the machine inched up my arm and squeezed tightly, all the way up to my shoulder. Mom came rushing down the stairs, released the rollers, threw a blanket around me, and dashed me to the hospital. I remember standing in a crib in this room, with large compresses on my arm. The accident left me with scars on my upper arm that have never left.

Another time I was rushed to the hospital, I was maybe eight or so. I had been excused from the dinner table, and everyone else was still sitting around it. I went into the bathroom and sat on the edge of the large sink, which happened to be filled with water, which I was told later could have been very serious. I'm not sure what possessed me, but one of the two light sockets had the bulb missing and I picked up one of Mom's hairpins and decided to see what would happen if I put it into the socket! Well, I soon found out! Sparks flew. The lights went off. And I had burns on my fingers and was again on my way across the bridge to the hospital.

Dad was quite a character and hard to keep up with. One never knew in which direction he was going, and often the staff at the mission were somewhat bewildered. As a child, I was a little abashed knowing this. It seemed that occasionally he had everyone going one direction and then without notice he had changed his mind for some reason and ended up going in the opposite direction.

Discipline was important to Dad and very likely one of the reasons he was able to accomplish all he did. When Mom had company over for a special evening or birthday celebration, he would excuse himself promptly at 10:15 to go to bed. All good Christians should be in bed by 10:30, he thought! Mom would be left to entertain the company, although no one likely would have stayed long after that polite but obvious departure.

Mom was the one who modified Dad. He had a real heart for helping people but, though he was generally wise, at times his soft heart led him in another direction. My first-grade teacher was a little unstable mentally, as mentioned earlier. She used to throw high heels at us; she kept them in the cupboard by her desk. Other times she threw books at us. And after her year of teaching us, she was put in a mental institute for a time. A few years later, she wrote Dad to ask if she could come back and teach again at the mission school. And Dad, who was always soft hearted and wanted to help, was ready to rehire her when Mom stated emphatically from the kitchen, "Herman, that woman is not going to teach our children!" Mom had had enough of her escapades and knew the results of her first round of teaching. Mom was generally gentle, kind, and soft-spoken, but she knew right from wrong and spoke up when it was necessary.

Mom and Dad had great respect for each other. Dad had respect for women in general, and I grew up thinking that it was normal for men and women to think highly of each other. I soon found out that was not the norm in the world, sad to say. Dad used to say, "Whatever a man can do, a woman can do better!" So it came as quite a shock to me to find the opposite attitude in the real world.

We are privileged to have had parents who loved each other and served the Lord all their lives. I think Mom will receive many jewels in her crown for her silent, faithful service as the wife of a busy medical missionary doctor on the rugged West Coast of Vancouver Island, raising eight children who mostly all love the Lord. She may not have received the accolades that Dad did, but God knows of her faithful service.

As a child, I felt a special connection to Dad. In every picture we have, I was on his knee. I think it was because of the intimate relationship I had with him as a baby when he came in many times throughout the day to see how I was. Of course, I have no proof of that but I always felt secure and had a special love for Dad. One day as he picked me up from high school, I asked him if he felt an extra something towards me. He said no! I'm not sure if that was so, or if he simply would not show favoritism.

At the end of his life, we had some special moments together. One day, I by now had two little boys, the youngest being 18 months old. Dad struggled in the hospital with depression and knowing his life was coming to an end. His heart which had been bad all his life was wearing out and he knew all the symptoms. He sat on the edge of his bed one day looking at his swollen ankles and said he thought he had had it. His heart was giving out. The nurses would often ask for a family member to stay with him at night. I was unable to because of the children, but this one day I came for a surprise visit at noon. The nurses had made him comfortable in the chair in his hospital room. When I unexpectedly opened the door, Dad looked up and said in the tenderest voice, "My dear little Lois." And I had a sense that, yes, there was something special between us.

As I grew into young adulthood, Dad wrote me letters, as I imagine he also did with the rest of the family. It of course was written in his typical medical scrawl, which took some effort to decipher. They were always letters of encouragement and admiration and love and advice for whatever the situation was at the moment. Stan also received one before we were married to let him know what Dad thought of his daughter, with wise advice on marriage and how he expected his girls to be treated. Those letters I still have among the things that are most treasured.

Another lesson I received from Dad was one day when our oldest boy was two. I had come down with a flu bug. Mom and Dad came to look after him for the day. By dinner time, I felt better and as they were leaving Dad said to me, "That little boy needs a spanking." Well, I had taken psychology in university and I knew better than to spank my children! I, being respectful, didn't say a word but it ate away at me. So after a few days, I called Dad up and related to him all the things I'd learned in psychology. "I didn't want my kids to obey me because I carried a great stick around to beat them with. I wanted them to obey because I was just so nice," I said. There was silence on the other end of the phone. Then Dad said, "Alright dear." And that was the end of the conversation. But I began to think. Who came first? The Bible or psychology? And I changed my mind about several teachings I had received. I've often thought of the wisdom my dad showed when he simply said, "Alright Dear." Both Mom and Dad had much wisdom and graciousness, although there was no room for misbehaving children!

Corporal punishment was a tool of training used occasionally in our home. It sounds so ominous, akin to execution! But it is a simple spanking. It had been the effective and acceptable form of discipline for hundreds, maybe thousands of years.

One day Dad was home with us and apparently we needed some discipline. Very likely for arguing, our favorite past time. We'd argue over who was going to begin making the double bed I shared with my younger sister. Because, you know, who ever begins has the greatest amount of work to do! So Dad sent us to our room and we waited by the bed. He came in with a spatula and told us to take off our rings which we laid on the bed. They he proceeded to spank us on each hand with the spatula – and had tears in his eyes. And I thought, "What a wonderful Dad" right in the middle of the spanking! His tears convinced me.

Poor Mom, on the other hand had to deal with us on a regular basis. She would thump out to the kitchen over the hardwood floors, in her sturdy house shoes, rummage around in the kitchen drawer for the strap and march right back into the bedroom where we waited. I used to think "Just wait till I grow up!" I'm not sure what I thought I was going to do when I did grow up. But neither of our parents ever lost their temper and although the spankings were felt no harm ever came from them.

Mission Ventures

Any free time Dad had was spent going out into the surrounding communities with the thought to hold a meeting and share the gospel message. When he went to the logging camps, he arranged to have the dining area in the cookhouse set up where he would bring a portable keyboard and possibly a projector to show a film to the men. He would then go around to the bunkhouses and invite the men to join him for the gathering. Generally there was someone with him to play the keyboard, or he would sit down and play it himself, singing hymns with the loggers out of the old hymn book. The favorite songs in those days that were often requested by the men were "The Old Rugged Cross" and "What a Friend We Have in Jesus." After singing and a message or a film, Dad put things back in order and made his way to the boat to get home before dark. Occasionally, he was invited to eat the delectable dinner that the loggers enjoyed.

At the local towns, he went into the bunkhouses to talk to the men and give out tracts or Shantyman papers. The loggers or the mill workers didn't always want to hear about anything spiritual. Some were pleasant and polite. Others were not so. I heard of one time a disgruntled logger called Dad a horse doctor. Dad, being able to stand his own ground with these burly men, shot right back at him, "I have to be a horse doctor to look after a bunch of donkeys like you!" You had to be tough to work on the coast.

Occasionally, he organized services in the First Nations villages. There was no large building on the grounds to hold a meeting, so he would arrange to have it in one of the larger homes. In the town of Zeballos, Dad set up

Sunday School for the children, and different staff members went to teach. Tahsis had a church, but Zeballos didn't, and the children enjoyed these services arranged for them.

In the summers, Daily Vacation Bible School (DVBS) was arranged for everyone, including the mission children. I spoke to Cathy Birtles the other day, who had been a staff member. She told me she had spent ten days teaching DVBS at a local town, and upon arriving home, Dad said there had been a request for another session at Muchalet. So he asked if she and a partner would go the next day, leaving no time to readjust or even find material for the session. But she graciously agreed, finding odd material in a room above the laundry that they sorted through as they made their way on the four-hour trip to Muchalet. Dad never let time and inconvenience stop him, and he sometimes expected the same of others.

The staff that came to the mission generally loved it. Cathy said in all her years of living, and even being on the foreign field, she valued her time at Esperanza as when she enjoyed life the most. She spent many years on the mission, working in the spiritual aspect of the mission and nursing in the hospital. She worked right alongside Dad, often assisting in the OR. She said he was jovial and pleasant to work with, loved what he was doing, and treated the staff as friends.

Cathy tells of one time she had a cyst that broke under her skin. It was near the front of her neck, and Dad said he wanted to open it up and clean it out. It had produced a large bruise that needed attention. So she was put in the upstairs hospital bedroom across from the OR, and as she waited there for surgery, Dad walked into the room with a large medical book under his arm and said, "I'm just studying up on my geography to be sure I don't nick your windpipe as I attend to your cyst!" She laughed. Dad could be quite a comic and witty, and knowing he was a good doctor, Cathy was not at all concerned.

As she continued chatting with me, she spoke of Dad's expertise in the maternity field. He was good with these ladies, and they wanted to come to him for the births of their babies. He was caring and understanding when it came to pain and suffering.

She related that Dad would examine the abdomen of an expectant mother as birth drew near, and if he found the baby not to be in optimum position for delivery, he massaged and worked on the baby's position until it was head down. He did this any time the situation wasn't right and seldom had to embark on a C-section.

He was an excellent surgeon, she stated, and very good at diagnosing without all the advantages today of being able to send a patient to a specialist. Cathy attended him in the OR, especially if manpower was short, as it often was. He used anyone willing to help and learn but ensured always the patient was in good care.

As the years went by, old staff members would gather wherever they were, at Three Hills for a conference or in town somewhere, to enjoy each other's company and reminisce of their days on the coast. We were often part of those gatherings, and they were precious indeed! We all enjoyed our time at Esperanza, and even those folks who came from the Prairies generally loved it. Occasionally, the isolation was too much for them, but once it got under your skin, it became a well-loved place to serve.

In later years, after I had left home and when Mom had moved to Sidney, Cathy states that Dad would take his breakfasts each morning with the staff at the hospital. Occasionally, he would tell Miss Parry the cook to take a Saturday morning off and he'd look after breakfast for the staff. He'd don his apron and make a huge batch of pancakes and spent the whole time happily flipping them on the stove while the staff ate. They loved it, and Dad loved making pancakes too.

Cathy and her husband had quite an experience one day as they were out rowing in a skiff towards CeePeeCee. The day was lovely, and they were enjoying themselves when they saw a pod of killer whales round the point and come in their direction. Thinking this seemed a little ominous, they rowed as quickly as they could towards the dock. The whales seemed to be coming right for them. They as quickly as possible made it to the wharf, climbed out, and watched as the whales came right up to the dock. They must have been hungry and thought they'd spied dinner. Cathy was relieved to be able to get out of the water and onto the dock. She said the fishermen told her that whenever a pod of whales came through the area, it was about five days before there were any fish around to catch. They wiped them out.

She related a comical situation with a new staff member from Eastern Canada. This new member was adjusting to life on the mission, when one day Cathy told her as she came on nursing duty at the hospital, "The Shantymen came in and were soaking wet. So I hung them up in the attic to dry." The new nurse wasn't sure what she was referring to but didn't ask any questions. Later, when she had a free moment, she decided to go up to the attic to see these Shantymen hanging out to dry, expecting maybe a very wet man? When she arrived, she found all the Shantymen papers hanging on a line, drying out just as Cathy had said. They had a good laugh about that.

Dad's Shipwreck

The story has been told in several other books, but I will include it here for those who haven't read about it.

Dad took a trip occasionally to the village of Kyuquot, as he did to all the villages around the area. Kyuquot was north of the mission. It was a white and Indigenous community and was a several hours journey by boat out around the mountains and into the open ocean. It is a treacherous voyage between rocks, seas, and all the dangers of the Pacific Ocean. As a child, I never went on that trip because I was afraid, but Mom and Dad did go occasionally together, and I remember Mom saying her knuckles were often white on a few of them, hanging onto the edge of her seat.

This particular fall, Dad had taken the *Messenger 11* (the ship that came before the Messenger 111) to Kyuquot to see to the medical needs there, as well as his missionary ventures. While he was there, a call came from Esperanza hospital that he was needed, so he left the boat tied up at the dock and flew back. Time was marching on, the days were getting shorter, and the likeliness of storms coming was increasing, so Dad felt he must get back to retrieve the boat before winter really set in.

Bruce, his 14-year-old son, and Garth, the younger son, both wanted to go, but for some reason, Dad allowed Bruce but not Garth. Possibly because of the age difference. So Bruce flew up with Dad to bring the boat back. Dad apparently had an ominous feeling about the whole trip but didn't mention it. When it was decided that the weather was fine, they embarked on this venture. Even at the best of times, this was a dangerous trip for a smaller boat.

Dad and Bruce were on their way. Things were fine at first, but it wasn't long before the wind began to howl, the waves whipped up, and they had a problem with the engine. Dad wasn't a mechanic, but he did what he could to fix the problem. There was one lifebelt on the boat, and Bruce offered it to Dad, but he insisted that Bruce wear it. Bruce was very seasick and spent most of the time lying on the bunk during all of this. However, both of them went out to the back of the boat for something, and as they were standing there, a huge wave lifted the boat, and they were flung out into the sea. Bruce had just said, "Dad, let's stick together."

Dad struggled in the wild ocean and at one point was under the boat and knew that if he didn't get a breath of air soon it would be over for him. He grabbed a hold of something, and it was Bruce's leg as he was tossed around in the waves. Just then a wave threw him up in the air, and he took a big gulp of air. He saw a rock nearby and did his best to manoeuvre over to it, hoping for a way to get out of the water. As he attempted to pull himself up, the waves continually pulled him back. If he had had the life jacket on, he said he wouldn't have been able to secure a good grip on the rock, but eventually he boosted himself out of the water. And on that rock is where he stayed for the next several days and nights wondering if the Lord was done with him or if He had more work for Dad to do. He never saw Bruce again. His last contact with him was when he grabbed a hold of his leg.

Dad tied himself to the rock so the waves wouldn't draw him back into the sea as they washed over him every minute or so. He was cold and weak from exposure and exhaustion. One day, as he waited there on that rock wondering about his future and scanning the sea, he spied a fish packer in the distance and waved wildly hoping to get their attention. Before long, he saw the ship turn towards him and he was filled with hope and joy. This boat rescued Dad from his awful situation. He climbed on board, the men gave him dry clothes, and he kneeled on the deck in tears and thanksgiving to the Lord. Maybe God was not finished with him yet. The packer took him home to Esperanza. No one there of course knew what had happened, but our little dog Spottie had at some point over those days gone to the beach facing west, the direction in which Dad was stranded, and howled and howled.

Dad went home and explained to Mom what had taken place. But there was a patient at the hospital waiting for surgery, so he changed into proper clothes and walked over to the hospital. Mom, in shock, threw on her coat and followed him right up to the OR, where she sat on a stool looking out over the channel. As Dad operated and Mom sat there on the stool, she had a vision of Bruce in the clouds over the channel and she knew he was safe at home in heaven. It brought comfort to Mom.

On the wall behind our piano in the living room was a plaque that read "Earth hath no sorrow that heaven cannot heal". It had been given to my folks at the time of this accident. I used to look at that plaque as it quietly bore witness to the truth that Mom and Dad experienced. They never talked a lot about the shipwreck or Bruce. They simply left God's doings in His hands and accepted what He brought into their lives.

Miracle Stones

I have often imagined an outdoor lamp standard in my backyard that has angular rocks piled to the top of the metal pole, and on each rock would be one word that reminded me of some miracle that the Lord has done in my life. Many of them small, but miracles just the same. And on those days, when you wonder, "Where are you, Lord? Do you see what's happening? Are you there?" I could walk out into my backyard and remember, yes, God did this miracle way back then, and yes, He also performed that one on that day, and yes, He is still here. Sometimes when my faith is small and even though I don't see Him or feel His presence right now, HE IS HERE!

Just like Joshua, when he and the Israelites crossed the Jordan River on dry ground, he told them to pile up rocks on the land so that when the younger generation asked about the pile of rocks, they could be explained as a symbol of the miracle that God had performed in a time of need. As of yet, I have not made a pile of rocks in the lamp standard in the backyard but I have made a collection for myself and the start of a collection for the youngest grandchildren, as each of them have had a miracle in their lives already.

Kai Lynn's miracle happened one day when she was about four years old. Her middle name, by the way, is Esperanza. Esperanza in Spanish means Hope. Her daddy is Columbian and speaks Spanish. It is a common name in Colombia and it sounds so melodic when he pronounces it with his accent. We were blessed when our daughter decided to use this for her second name.

Her miracle happened one day when I was taking care of her. I looked after Kai Lynn every Friday while her mom worked, and one afternoon I put her upstairs to bed on her mom's bed. After an hour or so, I thought I heard a little noise and wondered if she was awake. I was down on the lower floor folding laundry and continued on for a few more moments before I got up to check on her. Her dad was there on the couch with me, with his headphones on. As I walked along the hall by the side of the stairs, I heard a yell, and as I came around to the base of the stairs, I saw Kai Lynn falling in mid-air from the top. The landing was nothing but linoleum-covered cement, with no protective softness to ease the landing. I leaned over and kneeled on the bottom third step and caught her in mid-air. We all stood there quietly stunned, Kai Lynn in my arms. And we realized another miracle of God's gracious protection had just occurred. Had I folded one more piece of laundry, I would not have been there to catch her.

Logan's was somewhat different. I had been memorizing with the children the Psalm:

> I will bless the Lord who guides me,
> Even at night my heart instructs me.
> I know the Lord is always with me.
> I will not be shaken for He is right beside me.

That night, when Logan, who was about eight, went to bed, he dreamed that he and his sister and mom were standing out in a field in a terrible tornado. As they stood there everything around them was being affected but they were perfectly safe. In the morning, he asked his mom if that was the Lord protecting them all and "speaking" to him as the Psalm said. God speaks to us at times even through dreams, and I believe God was confirming His word to Logan that night.

After we moved to Edmonton from Victoria, one day a book from the Billy Graham Association came in the mail. I had not been in contact with them and hadn't supported them financially, but somehow this book arrived at my house.

Well, that book was my lifeline for the thirteen long years we lived in Edmonton. And God performed many miracles simply through that little book. When you read of the life of Mrs. Charles Cowman, the author of the book, she wrote the devotional during a very difficult time in her life. She and her husband had been missionaries but had to return home due to her husband's health. As she sat at home nursing him, she grieved that she could no longer be out serving the Lord but was rather stuck here in this situation. But that is when she began to write the words of this inspirational book. And I wonder how many hundreds of folks have been blessed and encouraged over the years by that book, written at a time when she felt that she was doing nothing for the Lord. It seems that God uses our difficult times and circumstances to His glory and the benefit of others.

Another miracle was the time when I made a move from working at the church office as secretary to the University of Alberta Hospital. I had found the church office to be a lonely job, and my husband, who worked at the U of A Hospital as an electrician, saw a posting for a position that seemed to describe me – able to work independently, transcribing doctors' reports, etc. – so I called the number on the notice. A lady by the name of Sharon answered, and when I told her about the posting, she said to come in the next day to see her. Taken aback, I replied that I had never taken medical terminology and had never transcribed medical doctors' reports. She said that was alright and to come anyway. I hung up the phone and was bewildered. Really? Me? No experience? And such a large hospital as the U of A?

Well, I went to the hospital, and Sharon sat me in front of a typewriter (before the age of computers) and gave me a tape of some doctor's dictation to transcribe. I was so nervous that I am not sure my fingers even hit the keys, and trying to understand, let alone spell, the medical words the unfamiliar voice was saying was a challenge indeed! Sometimes, a doctor's speech resembles their writing: it's hard to decipher. When enough time had elapsed, I took the sheet out and placed it on Sharon's desk. She didn't even look at it but asked me to come back the following Tuesday to see Dr. Medinsky, who was away on that day. So I returned the next week and had an interview with the doctor. She was very pleasant and asked if I would come back again the following Tuesday to see Dr. Nobert, whose office would be adjacent to mine in another building. The following Tuesday was Valentine's Day. And I was beginning to wonder, "Lord, you got me the job at the church. How can I leave it being your place of work? Can it really be you leading?" This had been very unusual, how it was happening, me without any medical terminology being accepted so quickly into the system of the U of A Hospital.

Well, that morning of the third interview, I opened my regular devotional written by Mrs. Cowman, and it read something to the effect, "God had called you there dear. Now He is calling you here. All His work will be done, so don't worry. Just go and accept this new calling!"

I could not believe it! Another mini-miracle by the Lord! And when I went for the final interview with Dr. Nobert, it was basically, well the office is yours if you would like it! And it was the best job I ever had. It is one of my miracle stones that I've placed in my special container.

As I write, I am reminded of a miracle that my mother had with my older brother Garth as a small baby. From the story Mom told, one day when Garth was about four months old, he began to cry and cry. Mom walked the floor with him day and night. This went on for quite a while. The doctors suggested Mom change his formula. But still he cried. Day and night, Mom carried the baby back and forth, and the only time he stopped crying was when he was exhausted and fell asleep. Mom began to get an ache in her upper back from the constant carrying and walking the baby that affected her the rest of her life whenever she tired. Finally, one day Mom and Dad asked Percy Wills to come over and pray for Garth. They all knelt together in prayer over him, and in a short time, he passed a date pit! Very likely given to him by his older brother who was trying to share his date treats with the baby. Mom could have had a miracle stone pile too!

There was also the sparrow miracle I related earlier. And it came into play again in our lives when we lost our 21-year-old son. I will relay that story later.

As a young person of 18 years of age, I began dating a young man from the church we attended. We went out for a year or two, and his masculinity and gentleness had taken my heart completely. He was a fine young man whose parents were very involved in the church and were upright godly folks.

One day, as summer vacation was upon us and just before we were to leave on a trip across Canada with my folks, he had taken me home from the Sunday evening service. Nothing was said. I just knew in my heart that this relationship was over. I spent a torturous night of tossing and turning. My heart was more than heavy. In the morning when I awoke, I stumbled out to the kitchen where we had a promise box on the windowsill above the sink. The promise boxes were small containers that held maybe 50 little cards, each with a promise on both sides. I picked randomly a card out of the box, and it read, "My son, give Me thine heart and let thine eyes observe My ways." And I knew the Lord was saying to me, I have another plan for you that does not include this man. Of course, I was devastated. We continued with our plans to drive across Canada, but Mom and Dad saw that I was in too much pain to continue, so they put me on a bus in Winnipeg, and I came home to stay with some dear family friends until their return.

Psalms 100 says that we are not our own. That we are the sheep of His pasture. He has a plan for each of us, and this was not His plan for me.

It was a couple of years later that I left home and was living in a little suite on the upper level of one of those old Victorian houses in Victoria, B.C., with a girlfriend. I had a job working on the medical ward of the Jubilee Hospital, and she was a practical nurse. One day, the phone rang, and another young man whom I had met was calling. He came over that night and after talking for some time in our little living room, we went out for coffee. As we drove home and he was parking the car on the lovely tree-lined street, the Lord spoke to me as clearly as anything I have ever heard from Him, "This is who you are going to marry." Just like that. I looked over at him parking the car. And that was the beginning of the relationship with my husband of more than 50 years.

There are many other stories of miracles that come our way. Sometimes it is simply a person who passes by and stops to say, "Are you a Christian? Because I felt God's spirit when I passed you!" This happened to me one day when I was sitting in a local coffee shop with my oldest grandson who was four. He was playing in the play area, and I had just sat down with my coffee and a muffin. As I sat there on this day that seemed rather blah, rainy, and with no particular spark, a lady carried her tray of food past me, stopped, turned around, and said to me "Are you a Christian? I felt God's spirit as I walked by you." And I thought, even on those dull almost depressing days, God's spirit is with us and can be felt by others.

Or another time when someone sitting in close vicinity at a local coffee shop says, "You have good energy" and I explain to them that the energy they are feeling is the Lord and explain salvation to them. The reason why these experiences mean so much is that the Lord is always with us, whether we feel His presence or not. Some of these times have been times of struggle that the Lord has worked His wonderful ways. It seems that God uses our times of struggle to teach us to walk in faith and remind us of His presence in each and every day of the lives of those who walk with Him in obedience.

Through waves and clouds and storms, He gently clears the way. Waves are the little difficulties we experience every day. Clouds are the days when nothing seems to be happening. And storms are those very difficult times that we experience. But in time, He clears the way. This is a little poem that Mrs. Cowman had written on the fly leaf of her devotional book.

It was winter of 1992, and we were preparing to leave Edmonton for our home province of B.C. As I sat in my chair and wondered what to share with my children upon departure, this verse came to mind, so I wrote it on a little note to each one of them. Look up and remember, "He gently will clear the way." Keep your eyes focused on "Him," the great captain of our ship. He is so wonderful. Look up! Look up! Look up!!

And when I look back years later, and see how God was preparing us for things that were coming, I am grateful. The truth of this verse has been proven. He has gently cleared the way in the storms that we have had in our lifetime.

Percy Wills

Uncle Percy, as Percy Wills was lovingly called by our family, had a tremendous impact on my life. Whenever the question is asked, "Who was the most influential person in your life?" my mind always goes to Uncle Percy. He was not a big man in stature but bigger than life in quiet influence. There was just something about his presence, his quiet beaming face, and his readiness to jump in and help whenever needed.

One Sunday we stopped in to visit Percy and Margaret in their home on the corner of Cloverdale and Quadra in Victoria. As we were welcomed by Percy, we entered the living room, and there was Margaret sitting quietly on the couch knitting! On Sunday! I was amazed and relieved as a teenager to find that a good Christian could knit on Sunday! After spending many years at Prairie High School with all their restrictions, and home where you could only go for a walk, have a picnic, or play a "Bible game" on the Lord's day, it was wonderfully freeing to find that you weren't quite so restricted. Now that I am older and understand the importance of what Mom and Dad and even Prairie were attempting to teach us, I realize it is a valuable lesson that perhaps today we need to practice more of – having respect for the Lord's day.

Messenger tied up at the hospital dock

At times, we would go along with these men, the Shantymen, for a boat ride to one of the local villages to visit and hand out Shantyman papers. At the end of each visit and after a cup of tea had usually been served, everyone gathered around the kitchen stove on the way out the door and stopped to have a word of prayer before leaving the family. Then we stopped at a few more homes before we boarded the boat to return home.

One story is told of a time when Uncle Percy knocked on the door of an isolated home to have the door opened by a very tired looking young mom with a baby on her hip and a toddler clinging to her knees. Noticing that the fire was almost out and the wood box empty, he went outside, cut enough wood to fill the box, and relighted the fire. When that was done, as the house was warming up, he went over to tackle the mound of dishes that were strewn over the kitchen counter.

Many times, as a young girl, I watched as the visiting Shantymen donned aprons around their ample middles, one with his hands in the "dishpan" and the others with tea towels in hand, singing, chatting, and visiting as they did up the dinner dishes. Uncle Percy used to joke about his ample middle.

When folks said he needed to keep an eye on his waistline, he said he kept it out where he *could* keep his eye on it!

It was a surprise to me after I grew up and was out in the "real" world that I found that men helping with dishes was not normal. When I think of wonderful men, I think of the Shantymen and my Dad, who also had this wonderful habit. They didn't sit in the living room while the ladies worked in the kitchen. No, they got right in there themselves with their sleeves rolled up and had a marvelous time while they did it.

Those men really knew and depended on the Lord. And I have heard it said, and believe it is true, that the closer a man is to God, the better he treats his wife. Each of these men, including my father, treated their wives like queens.

It was a privilege to have Percy and Dad marry Stan and I in Victoria in April 1969. We were saddened to hear of his death in 1990 while we lived in Edmonton. He apparently had stretched out on the couch for an afternoon nap and "woke up in heaven," as his daughter Darda Burkhart says in her book, *Forging Ahead for God*. We had not heard of his death until a few months later so were unable to attend his funeral. It was just like Uncle Percy to have little made of himself, and I never heard much of his funeral service. Dad's funeral also seemed unpretentious. Both men were humble servants of the Lord. Percy was at Dad's funeral service several years earlier, and when it was over, Uncle Percy returned to his car in the lot across the street to find his tire flat. Instead of the usual complaints that most of us would spurt, Percy stood up after looking at the tire, looked around the parking lot, and said, "There must be somebody here God wants me to talk to."

It was an honour to read that Dad was included right along with such a man of God in the comment made by the officiating pastor at his funeral: "The names of Johnson, Wills, Peters, and McLean will shine in glory like gold on black velvet." What treasure has been ours to be associated with him! We look forward to the wonders of heaven and reuniting with these beloved saints.

Friendly Cove

There were three local Indigenous villages within a day's boat trip from Esperanza. All of them were situated in the most beautiful locations you could imagine, couched by the sea on all sides and windswept beaches. Friendly Cove was the most beautiful. It was set in a cove on a knoll that rose gently up and over to the open ocean that faced Japan. The rollers swept in and rolled the driftwood around with each sweep. The sand had been ground to a fine texture by the continual action of the sea. And there was always a breeze off the ocean. The bay or cove on the other side of the knoll where we anchored the boat was somewhat protected, but still there were gentle swells that had to be manoeuvred to get to shore. The lifeboat was taken off the roof as usual, and after everyone on board climbed in, we rowed into the pebbly beach, timing our arrival with the swells so as not to capsize our little craft. Occasionally, Dad did have some episodes of being dumped in the "salt chuck," medical grip and all, from which he had to recover to continue on his mission up to the village.

Several times, I attended Dad on these trips, along with whomever else from the mission came. The homes were built in a row along the top of the knoll facing the cove. The ones I was in seemed to be just one large room, with double beds covered in tufted colorful quilts lined up against the back wall, a woodburning stove in the middle, and a family-sized table by the picture window looking out at the cove. There was a lighthouse on the rocks to the entrance of Friendly cove, so the view from these homes was magnificent. I would follow Dad up the worn dirt pathway strewn with fish heads and spines, and he would be welcomed into the home. As we sat with the folks at the kitchen table, all the neighbour kids and dogs ran in and out freely, whether or not the home belonged to them. Grandma Jumbo's home was the one I remember best. She was a First Nations woman who I imagine lived all her life there at Friendly Cove. Dad visited always handing out the Shantyman newspaper that was filled with inspiring stories, and of course, he treated any medical needs that might be needing attention. If the condition required hospitalization, he would bring the patient along to the boat and back home to Esperanza, which usually was about a two-hour ride.

The stoves in the center of the homes were often a cause of fires and severe burns for the folks of the village. I remember one girl who had apparently thrown gasoline on the fire, and she caught on fire. She was admitted to the hospital and was covered in burns on most of her body. I remember a large, wooden, rounded support that was placed over her bed to keep the covers off of her painful burns. I don't know how many months she was there recovering, but I do remember seeing her years later with severe scars on the front of her neck that kept her from raising her head. Another family's stove fire consumed the whole house and several of the family members along with it. Tragedies of this sort were all too common in the villages.

One time while we were at Friendly Cove, I remember visiting a home on the north end of the row of houses. I seemed to be there by myself in my memory, standing in the kitchen. The mother of the home was baking bread, and she pulled out some warm, fresh white bread from the oven, and before I knew what was happening a number of kids and teenagers materialized around the kitchen table, slicing and slathering with strawberry jam the wonderful smelling bread. I stood there. No one invited me to sit with them, and I somehow never even thought of or expected it. I just watched in amazement at how the kids materialized in such silence. They always had a quiet, thoughtfulness about them.

The Indigenous women were wonderful bakers. They made the most short, delicious pastry. They did skilful beadwork and basket weaving. We often were given gifts of lovely woven baskets with the whale or other logos neatly woven into the design. We would be gifted with the little beaded men and women they were so crafty at making. Other times we received lovely crocheted doilies. We watched them make their Indian sweaters that also had their patterns of wildlife on them. One year, Mom made us each one for Christmas, but I found that although the wool was warm, the wind whistled right through the knitted stitches, which made it cold to wear.

Several years later, I had an interesting experience when an Indigenous family that was part of the mission had invited me to go along with them to Friendly Cove for an "Indian Sports Day." I had never heard of the Indigenous having a sports day. But as their 16-year-old son was my first boyfriend, I went along on their trawler for the two- to three-hour ride to the village. I don't remember a lot about the trip. I just remember after we arrived, the whole family deserted me, and I roamed around Friendly Cove alone. I was the only white person there, unless the priest was around. But I didn't see him. Were they embarrassed that I was white and the only white person there? I don't know. The return trip was uneventful, and the situation was never mentioned.

Several years later, that same boyfriend came all the way from the West Coast to visit us after we had moved from Esperanza to Sidney, B.C. I think he was wondering if there was still something between us for a future together, but high school had passed and the natural changes that came along with it, so he went home and I never saw him again. I had heard several years later that his family had experienced a house fire that took the lives of several of his family members.

He and his siblings attended the Residential School on the island as school children. I realize that there is much said about Residential schools and the negative effects they had on some children. Many children were dreadfully hurt by wrongs done by the organizations that started them. But I think we should also acknowledge the good that was accomplished by many others and that there were many children who looked forward to going in the fall.

These Natives we knew enjoyed attending the school, and I have heard that many of the parents did as well. They were able to come with their fishing boats and tie up at the school called Christie and enjoy a meal with their children or teenagers. There were no organized sports or activities on the reservations, and with rain a staple, the kids were surrounded by mud and no outlet of interest other than fishing off the dock with their fishing lines. You would see them sprawled out on the dock peering into the water around the pilings watching for fish. So going to Christie was a positive experience, and one they looked forward to come fall.

Mother

"A virtuous woman, who can find? Her worth is far above rubies." Mother was a woman of strength and dignity, virtuous and kind, full of wisdom. She was queenly and most refined. A real lady. Being on the rugged West Coast did not deter her from keeping a lovely warm home and herself in ladylikeness and refinement. Behind every great man is a great woman, and Dad couldn't have spent 37 years on the West Coast without Mom being a faithful partner by his side.

Mom and I and Spottie

As a child, I wasn't especially close to Mom. There was one child after me – the baby of the family – and whether that was the cause of the distance in our connection or whether it was simply that I was more like Dad in being somewhat independent, not as expressive in my feelings as my younger sister was, there was just a distance between us and what I felt was a misunderstanding. However, there was never any doubt that we were all loved. And generally treated fairly.

In later years, Mom and I became very close. She came out to visit us each year after we moved to Edmonton and stayed with our family for a six-week stint at a time. Mom seemed very content while she was with us. We gave her a room just off the kitchen, where she sat and wrote her life story and enjoyed the happy sounds of family life with the kids coming and going and me doing the usual homemaking things mothers do. And I enjoyed it too. When she left, generally in the fall, I had a difficult time readjusting to winters alone as a stay-at-home mom in a city that had winter from October to April, or so it seemed to me. On one of those visits, Mom had graciously apologized for the misunderstanding and difficulties I had experienced as a child. She had been unaware of what was going on behind the scenes with children who can be cunning and sneaky. I thought it was most gracious of Mom to be willing to acknowledge that.

There is a story that has been passed down about Mother's ancestry. It seems that a few generations back, when her family lived in England, a baby was left on the doorstep of her family's home. No one knew anything about this child, but it appeared to be wrapped in the clothes of royalty. When that child grew up, it resembled Queen Victoria, and my mother herself looked very much like Queen Victoria. Nothing has ever been proven, but it does appear as though there is some heritage there. Mom was also queenly, refined, and quite English in her ways. Of course, her heritage was Irish, English, and what Mom called Pennsylvania Dutch. So she always told us she had Dutch blood in her. I have learned recently that the Dutch originated in Germany, and many generations ago, they left to settle Holland due to religious differences. We also, interestingly, have a connection to Elvis Presley on my father's side. It was traced to an aunt who went to the United States years ago and married a Presley. We are apparently fifth cousins to Elvis.

I have wonderful memories of Mom. One is coming home from school on a bright, sunny spring day and finding Mother sitting in the living room, dressed in her grey, pinstriped worsted skirt and a lovely, white eyelet blouse, entertaining some staff ladies with afternoon tea. The blinds were pulled to keep out the intensity of the sun, and Mom's cheeks were flushed and her silver, wavy hair was up as she always wore it. She sat primly chatting with the ladies over fruitcake and teacups and saucers. She would let us have a cup of tea in her china with milk and sugar, and I enjoyed the whole affair.

Other days, especially Mondays as they were wash days, we came home from school to find Mom standing by the wood cook stove in the kitchen preparing supper, only we couldn't see her as she was behind the laundry that was drying on the rack in the middle of the kitchen. It was a rack that she lowered from the ceiling, hung her wet wash on, and then pulled it back up. But only the bottom of her dress and shoes were visible until she came out from behind the clothes and greeted us. The windows would be steamed up with the moisture in the kitchen. Her cheeks again rosy.

Each day after Mom had done her housework, she would prepare dinner over the stove, set the table by the window, and when all was ready, she always went back into her bedroom, powdered herself, put on a fresh dress, and tidied her hair for dinner. And there she sat at the end of the table looking like a very dignified lady, pouring tea from the teapot and enjoying supper with us as we chatted about the day's happenings. Dad, of course, was always there unless he was held up at the hospital or by poor weather on one of his weekly outings to the local towns in the *Bruce*. The odd time that he came home late, Mom would fry up some eggs and sit with him while he ate.

One day when my younger sister and I were home, and it seemed no one else was around, Mom told us she was going to prepare a special dinner for the three of us and we weren't allowed in the kitchen. When it was finally ready, Mom had pulled the kitchen table over by the warm stove on this cold winter night and had bacon and eggs all prepared, a real special treat for us.

Mom often told us the story of how she became aware of Dad's interest in her. They were neighbors on farms in Saskatchewan – the Cards and the McLeans. One night, the Cards had invited the McLeans over for dinner. But just as dinner was about to be served, one of those Prairie storms came up, and Mom was needed to go out to gather the cows in from the pasture.

By the time she came back home, her long, wavy, auburn hair was soaking wet, so she ran up the stairs to tidy herself for dinner. The company was already seated when she came down the stairs to join them. When the meal was over, Mom began to clear the table and went into the kitchen to begin doing dishes. It wasn't long before Dad left the company in the dining room and joined her in washing up. A habit that Dad continued as long as I can remember – helping with the dishes. Mom said while they were doing the cleanup, Dad looked at her in such a way that she knew he had a real interest in her. Mom was nine years younger than Dad. And he waited for Mom until he was 28 and she was 19. That day in the kitchen was the beginning of a long courtship. Their first date was when Mom was 16, the earliest that she was allowed to date, and Dad sent her up in an airplane. He had only enough money for one ride, $10, so he didn't accompany her. They were married on the Prairies on December 22 a few years later. I remember them talking about how bitterly cold it was that day and that Dad made biscuits for breakfast on his wedding day. Mom spoke of a beautiful warm coat she had purchased for the occasion. It cost $100, which was a lot of money in the 1920s. As they boarded the train for their honeymoon, some jokester friend knocked Dad's hat off, which led to an awful cold. Not much was related about the honeymoon except one time Dad mentioned with a twinkle in his eye that they slept in until two in the afternoon, a highly unusual event for my parents, and Mother said, "Oh, Herman!" with very flushed cheeks. And after more than 50 years of marriage, Dad still wrote wonderful sweet notes and cards to Mom, often addressing her as "Sweetheart."

For the years before I came along and the early years of the mission operation Mom was involved in every aspect from making meals for the small staff and those first patients to anything that was needed to make it operate smoothly.

By the time we younger ones were on the scene Mom's role was that of the doctor's wife. She had no particular role at the hospital but was involved in any activity that came along. Her time was taken up with keeping house for a busy man and her family of eight, who were spread out over four decades. Home was a refuge for Dad who sometimes trudged over the bridge and up the back steps, his feet almost too heavy to climb the stairs, exhausted from his hours of work at the hospital.

She followed her own schedule that included wash days on Mondays, Tuesdays with Dad on the boat to Tahsis, Thursdays were days for cleaning bed linens when we took off the bottom sheet of our bed and replaced them with the top sheet, and then another fresh one on top. And Fridays were her clean the house days. Because our floors were hardwood everywhere except the kitchen and bathroom she swept and dusted with a dust mop, then waxed them with a paste wax and polished them by hand on her hands and knees. As a child I noticed as she got older – she was in her 50s by the time I was in elementary school – that what used to take her until lunch time to finish now took her all day so that when we came home for a hot meal at noon the house was upside down in the process of being cleaned. Later our first vacuum arrived. It was certainly noisier than a dust mop. And a floor polisher appeared too and Mom no longer had to be on hands and knees polishing her large hardwood floor.

Our home was across the bridge which seemed to slightly separate it from the hospital. And Mom seemed to me to be like a lighthouse over there on her piece of property – quiet, steady, very noticeable, her presence felt by the staff and visitors, giving out quietly her beam of light which was faithfully grounded on the Rock. There was a sense of respect for Mom and she was known as Mrs. McLean although in later years she was often called Mother McLean by staff members and friends.

One of the staff members became an extra special friend to Mom. Mrs. Plummer was a woman of prayer. She had the gift of the heavenly language which was not common on the mission. No one was ever against it, it just didn't happen often. Her soft brown eyes exuded warmth and love. Her face seemed enveloped in a glow.

One day Mom asked Mrs. Plummer if she would pray about her watch which she had lost. So Mrs. Plummer did. When she went to bed that night she dreamed that there was a large can outside full of rain water and in the bottom of the can was a watch. So next morning when she awoke, she got up, dressed and went outside looking for a can somewhere on the grounds. And sure enough she found a can full of rain water and in the bottom was Mom's watch! God answered her prayers.

One day in later years Mom was listening to a program about Oral Roberts, who had founded a university in the southern states and was a well known evangelist. She wasn't a particular fan of Oral Roberts but she heard someone criticizing him and she quietly said "Don't criticize a man God has called". Mom often spoke quiet words of wisdom.

And I thought of that in later years when I heard Dad being unceremoniously lumped in with Colonialists. I was glad that Mom and Dad weren't around to hear that. If they had been I imagine Mom would have made a quiet comment to us at home. Dad would have said nothing and left it all in the Lord's hands, as he did with all criticisms that came his way.

Dad did feel that everyone needed an education. He did speak to everyone in English, the universal language, whether their mother tongue was Swedish, Italian, or French. He did teach habits that would enhance good health. He thought that discipline and order were qualities that made for a productive life. And he was aware of negative spiritual influences that were practised over the years. If that is the definition of a Colonialist then maybe he was one.

Often other doctors would come to the coast to help out with the mission medical work. One young doctor and his wife had come to help Dad out in the hospital. They stayed for several years and had their first two children at Esperanza. I often babysat for their two little girls. But one day they decided it was time to leave and as Mom held a farewell party for them, the wife stood up and with tears addressed Mom saying she didn't know how Mom could endure the long hours without her husband and the years she had spent in this difficult situation that was really too much for her to endure. It was a testimony to Mom's faithfulness, stability and steadfastness.

As I think of the way God graciously took both my parents home at the end of their lives, I am thankful. Psalms 116:15 says "Blessed in the sight of the Lord is the death of His saints" or another translation puts it "He tenderly cares for His who are dying".

We had special times with them both at the end. The night before Dad died, we were up at the Jubilee Hospital in Victoria visiting him with Mom. He commented on her hot pink top and that it was a favorite blouse of hers. As the bell went to notify us that visiting hours were over, we held Dad's hand, us on one side of the bed and Mom on the other, and Dad prayed. His voice was weak. I think his oxygen was low. But he thanked God as if he was sitting in His presence, that he had spent his whole life serving Him on the coast. At 5 am the next morning, the hospital called to say that Dad had gone home.

A Tribute to Nurses

After the call came from the hospital that Dad was gone we quickly dressed and arrived to find him laying in bed, his hands folded and his covers straightened by the attending nurses. He looked peaceful and natural. We put our hands on his and kissed him with tears streaming down our faces.

The nurses went quietly around the room doing their duties, with tears in their eyes. They realized how much this father meant to his family. Perhaps they had learned to love him too over the time they had looked after him as he died. They had spent the night caring for him.

Nurses, you are a blessing from God. Your gentle touch, your calming voice, your quiet dedication to those in your care bring silent comfort to both patient and those who love them.

You are God's angels. You are God's touch. You are God's blessing to those you comfort. May God bless you abundantly with His presence, His peace and His comfort as you comfort others in their time of need.

A Shoe Story

We had moved to Edmonton from Victoria after our three children were born. It was a company move, and we expected it would not be permanent. Moving from the beautiful West Coast to Edmonton! Well, I always said it took me seven years to adjust. It was very difficult to move totally away from family and the loveliness of B.C. The Lord taught me a lot while I was there. Learning to trust Him, even in the dark.

I had taken a job at the Woodward's shoe department because I needed to get out of the house and be with people, as I was a stay-at-home mom. The older boys were in school, and our youngest daughter was looked after by a good and trusted friend.

I had only been at the store a few months when Stan was told he was laid off and the company that moved him to Edmonton was closing. This happened a few days before Christmas in the middle of an Edmonton winter. What a disastrous shock that was! No family. No work. And my imagination ran wild as I imagined us sitting around our family table with nothing to eat and the house freezing cold in the Alberta winter!

During the first few months at the store, I had spied a lovely pair of shoes that we had in stock. They came in all colors, from black to brown to grey to ivory, and in patent leather and suede, and in my spare time, I would go to the stockroom, climb on a ladder, and get a pair of grey suede ones in 7½ B just to try on for fun. They were lovely. But they were $54 and that was just too much, especially unthinkable now that Stan was out of work.

One day, I jokingly said to my supervisor, "Why don't you let me take a pair of Grey Gypsies (the name of the shoe) home for the weekend, and I will bring them back on Monday?" Well, he said, have you looked on the shelf where returns are stored? I didn't know there was a shelf where we kept returns. So I went back to look, and there were maybe a couple of shoes there, and if you can imagine, there was a pair of Grey Gypsies 7½ B!!! I couldn't believe my eyes! And my boss said, "You can have them for $2!"

This little episode was a lesson it seemed from the Lord. A lesson that said, "You don't NEED a pair of Grey Gypsies, but I care about you – even the little things – and I want to bless you, especially during this time of doubt and difficulty with Stan being out of work." It seemed a confirmation that the Lord knew and would look after us.

Several years later, after we had moved back to B.C., this shoe story took another interesting turn. I was part of a ladies Bible Study, and we were out for a Christmas luncheon at a golf course. Each of us had a small gift to bless another lady with, and each of us were to direct the receiver of our gift to do some small thing, like go over to those golfers and wish them a Merry Christmas. Well, among our group was a lady who was a little different. Odd perhaps? And she had a gift for me. She was to tell me what little thing I was to do before she gave it to me, and wouldn't you know it, this little lady decided she had to pray about it!! We all looked at each other and waited while she prayed silently with her head bowed. When she was finished, she looked up at me and said, "Tell me a shoe story!" And I thought, God can use even strange little old ladies – and even me if I am just willing to listen! So I related my shoe story.

Our Son Grant

Grant was our oldest child, the eldest of three. He became, as he grew, a rather unusual boy in his politeness, his scholastic abilities, and his popularity among almost everyone. He had been a blessing to us as parents and caused us no trouble, that is until he turned 17. And actually it was fairly normal, as I look back on it now, but as the mother of a first child and trying to be the best mother there ever was, not too strict and not too lenient, it came as a great painful shock to realize that in spite of all my efforts, he rebelled at 17.

Our first indication of a little trouble was when he was about ten. He was a slightly built boy, and one morning when I was in the bedroom curling my hair, he came in and said, "Mom, I really think Todd needs another spanking." Todd was his brother, about two years younger. Well, our son Todd had received his share of discipline. So I stopped my hair curling and sat in the rocking chair in the bedroom, pulled Grant on to my lap, and explained to him that his brother had had his share of discipline and that for now I didn't think he needed any more. At least for the time being. Grant got up off my lap and from then on had an attitude of resentment that we were never able to help him overcome. However, he kept it under his hat, always obeyed but we could see it there in his eyes.

One day during teacher/parent interviews when Grant was in Grade 6, we walked into the classroom to find two teachers standing, eagerly awaiting our arrival. When we entered, they said, "Well, here are the parents of this unusual student," and I was taken aback. He was a wonderful child, but I'm not sure it was because of us.

Another time in high school, the principal decided that if you treat students like adults and let them make their own decisions, they will act responsibly. A move and belief of psychology that I didn't agree with. So they allowed the kids to decide whether or not they wanted to attend class, do their homework, etc. I was totally against this policy, but the school implemented it at the beginning of the year. So at times, Grant would come home and say, "Mom, my friend needed counselling so I skipped class." One day, I received a call from the school to say that our son had skipped ten classes and what was I going to do about it. And I replied, why are you calling me? It is your policy, not mine. And shortly thereafter, the principal was replaced and so was the policy of allowing teenagers to make all of their own decisions!

Grant took music lessons, as all of our children did. He got to eighth grade Royal Conservatory but was struggling with interest and the desire to practice. So to give him incentive, I said that if he completed the work and exam for eighth grade, we would send him on a special trip to see my oldest brother, his Uncle Max who lived in Indiana. Money was scarce with only one working parent and three children to raise, but we made the promise and intended to keep it.

Well he practised and did write the exam. At about the same time, there was a competition going on federally among the high school students, and four young people from across Canada would be chosen for it. Grant turned out to be one of the students chosen. And the four of them would be sent - to Indiana for the event! So we were once again blessed with an unusual circumstance. Grant went with the kids and we made arrangements for him to stay longer to have a visit with his uncle and cousins. They took him to the Indianapolis car races and he had a wonderful experience with that side of the family. And we didn't have to pay a penny.

During Grant's 17th year, he began to stay out overnight at friends' homes, unknown to us. It seemed to be something the kids in Edmonton were doing at that time. We would occasionally wake up in the morning to another boy sleeping in our sons' rooms because they were upset with their parents. I always talked to the boys and let them know that their parents loved them, and they needed to call them right away to at least let them know where they were. And Grant began to rebel in other ways. I found it unbelievable and very disturbing. That year, I read over and over in the Living Bible in Philippians 4, "Don't worry about anything. Instead pray about everything." I highlighted it in green and reminded myself over and over – don't worry about anything. One day I called around to see if there was any counsellor I could talk to about the situation, as we had no family to share these difficulties with. And I came across Catholic Social Services in the phone book. The man on the other end of the line, hearing this upset mother, said that if I came to his office before the building closed, he would stay and talk to me as long as I needed. What kindness! I had not received that kindness when I called the local Christian counselling service I'm afraid. So we went. And a man named Don Freeman came and warmly welcomed us into his office. I related tearfully the situation with our son, and when I was done, he said, "It sounds to me like you have a wonderful son!" The relief of that comment brought peace to my soul. I very likely wasn't thinking straight and was overly emotional in the situation. I have never forgotten that wonderful man and here 30 years later I remember his name and kindness.

During this time, Grant had decided he never wanted to step inside a Pentecostal church again. We had gone to one in Edmonton for most of our time there. It was a good church, with wonderful music, and I worked in the church office for a couple of years. However, it was a German Pentecostal, and I always said, we were neither German nor Pentecostal so none of us really fit in, not even Grant who was most outgoing and likeable. So the result was that he chose as his friends non-church kids. He would bring them home, and we would have eight or ten sitting together in our family room watching movies or going out to play street hockey, or in the summer, we would find them bouncing basketballs down the street in the middle of the night! But of course, this was a real concern to me as the kids, even though very nice, did not have the values I had tried to instill in ours.

Well, in the fall of 1991, Stan had gotten a job back in B.C. – something I never dreamed would happen. What a wonderful blessing after all those difficult years in Edmonton. We were overjoyed. The boys were living together in an apartment, both working, Grant driving the stretch limousines and, if I remember right, Todd was managing an Esso station. Kari Lee, our daughter, was boarding at Prairie High School and so in January 1992, we packed up our home in Edmonton and made the move to the Vancouver area. We had left out a few special dishes for our last Christmas Eve together, and I remember Grant picking up the tray of Christmas tree buns I always made and as he carried them into the dining room, he said, "Mom, you should really sell these buns." Christmas Eve was always the highlight of the season for us. We set the table with all the goodies, home baked of course, turned off all lights other than candles and Christmas lights, and enjoyed a wonderful evening together. This was a tradition that Mother had started when I was a child, and we kept it going.

Our move was spectacular. At least that is how we felt. Oh to be back home in B.C. God had answered our prayer for a "perfect little spot" by finding us a home in Fort Langley, which we enjoyed for 23 years.

Grant had come out to visit us in the summer of that year. In typical Grant style, he rented a Mustang convertible and took each of us for rides. When it was my turn, he turned his CD player on and played the Beach Boys, thinking that might please me and be from my era, as he drove along Glover Road by the lowland golf course. He was always a delight. Everyone was happy to see and be with him.

Well, the time for his departure came, and it happened to coincide with a train trip we had planned to Squamish. He was unable to come along, so we said our goodbyes and left him at home. When we returned, he was gone. The house was empty. And on the table was a gift wrapped in brown paper. I had an eerie feeling about it. I opened it quietly and found a lovely picture of a single bird, sitting alone on a branch. A sparrow? It seemed that way to me. And I thought of that special verse in the Bible about how God sees the sparrow and how much more He cares about us.

Well, we heard from him often over the next months. And I began to feel my heart stop each time the phone rang, and I would breathe, "Oh, God." Not sure why but just had a feeling that took my breath away. And the last call we had, he said, "Mom, I have good news and bad news. The good news is that I got Todd a job driving limo. The bad news is that I have been turned down to attend SFU as they are taking students from in-province first." Apparently soon after that, one day in Edmonton, he and a friend, Meridith, went out to a field at night. He offered her his jacket because it was cold and as he sat there in the field on his basketball, he said to her, I don't know why but God doesn't want me to go to the Vancouver area. And they decided that He must have another plan. And He did.

Well, November 13 of that year, I was sitting in my usual spot in the morning having my usual devotions. But this day, my Bible was open to Philippians 4, highlighted in green, reading and praying and remembering the difficult time I had had when Grant was 17. He was 21 now, so it was several years later, and as was my custom, I read the Bible from Genesis to Revelation, over and over, and today, of all things, here I was reading the portion that was "Grant's" portion. Stan was upstairs sleeping, another unusual event, because he was on night shift.

The phone rang, and I answered it. It was Dave, another limo driver that we had known in Edmonton. "Mrs. Hooks? Grant has been in a single car accident." "Is he OK?" I asked. "No." " Please hold on," I said while I took the phone up to Stan in bed. I couldn't face what was about to be stated so I gave the receiver to Stan. I heard, no he is not alright. Stan choked. And he hung up the phone. And that began another reality in our life.

Numbly, we went about our business. Knowing we had to be strong for Kari Lee who was in high school back in B.C. She hadn't been able to return to the same boarding home she had been in, in Alberta so she returned to B.C. for this year of school, which turned out to be a blessing with these circumstances we were now facing.

We had spent 13 long years in Edmonton and had learned to cope on our own. We somehow didn't even think there would be any outside help or support. So we went to the school and got permission to pick up our daughter from class. On the way out the door of the school, we relayed the news to her. She like us was quiet and numb. I think that the reality of these kind of situations would be more than a person's heart could manage and that the numbness is a sort of protection.

The first tears came when my sister showed up at the door. That was the first realization that there was support, and it softened me to the point of feeling and not having to be strong. Well, we packed up and were on our way to Edmonton, playing the Gaithers all the way. The limo company arranged to put us up in a hotel, since the accident happened while he was driving. When we arrived in the room, there was a large basket of fruit and notes on the table from Grant's Bible Study group, who had just met the night before. Apparently, they said, Grant had been noticed singing the song, "Oh, Lord you're beautiful, Your face is all I see." And he seemed to be off and not present in the room. Kind of in another realm. They told us of another night that after everyone had left the study, and the parents of the home were upstairs tending the children, they came down to find Grant in the kitchen doing up the dishes. He was an unusual boy.

The "kids" or friends of the boys were heart-broken. We went up to our son's apartment, and they all sat around us in silence. We went into Grant's bedroom and saw his clothes hanging in the closet, each hanger exactly two inches apart. He was meticulous. A few days later, when we returned to the apartment, the clothes were gone. It seemed the kids took it upon themselves to make all the arrangements, and oddly they seemed to think we didn't need to be involved. However, I was aware of their pain too. And when I went on the day of the funeral, very early to be with Grant's body for a while, here the kids were already there. I felt that they needed time with him too, so I quietly let it be.

There were hundreds at his funeral. Folks were sitting on the platform, because they ran out of room. A journalist from the *Edmonton Journal* newspaper was there and gave a reading about Grant. Apparently, Grant had driven him home via limo and rather than just dropping him off, he accompanied him up to the apartment, unlocked the door for him, and made sure he had everything he needed as he was wheelchair bound, before he said goodbye and left.

His grade six teachers wrote me letters about their wonderful, unforgettable student, Grant. I heard from the teenagers. And wonderful to say, God used this to bring most if not all of those unchurched teenagers to Himself through Grant's death.

The day after our arrival in Edmonton to make arrangements for his funeral, we decided to take a ride down to the area south of the city where the accident had happened. It had occurred in the early morning after he had dropped a customer off at the airport. He apparently had pulled the limo over to the side of the road and a farmer in the neighboring field noticed him. After a few moments he drove down the road and where the road turned, he didn't, and he and the limo ended up in the field. He was thrown out of the car as they were advised not to wear seat belts, and apparently the limo rolled over him.

We stopped at the sight. We stood in silence. How could it be? We could see tire marks on the road as if he had tried to apply the brakes. Stan went down into the field and retrieved some of his notes that were tossed out during the accident. And we found his shoes. And I remembered someone had told me that when you are unconscious your shoes fall off. That thought came to me as a comfort thinking that perhaps Grant had been quite unaware of the situation and therefore didn't suffer. As we drove away on the road that we knew very well, we looked up and for the first time, we saw the name of the road. **Sparrow Road.** Sparrow Road?! Really? Another example of God's tender loving care and reminder that He is there even in the most tragic of affairs. His eye is on the sparrow – so He was aware of everything that happened to us and to Grant.

Well, the next weeks and months and years it took for us to adjust to our new reality. We brought his body home and buried him in the Fort Langley cemetery. On his tombstone, we wrote:

Precious son. Cherished brother. Dear to us all.

God knows best. We will trust Him.

And for the next several years, each Christmas Eve we would go down as a family and put a candle on his grave. It had been one of his favorite times of the year. We put candles out on our walkway and gave each member of the family a candle to remember Grant by. We would stand by his grave and sing "But until then, our heart will go on singing," a Gaither song, and then pray before returning to the house for our Christmas Eve.

Yes, God knows best. We do our best to trust Him. Sometimes we need reminding of this when life gets difficult. I just wrote on a recipe card the words from that old song, "What a Friend We Have in Jesus." The lines I wrote are:

> Oh! what peace we often forfeit,
> Oh! What needless pain we bear
> All because we do not carry
> Everything to God in Prayer.

Kids Say the Funnest Things

Children between the ages of two and four come up with the funniest comments. Or they just do the funnest things. I have a book for each of my grandchildren that I have written a few of them in for a keepsake.

One Sunday, we had Dionte, our oldest grandson, in church, and I'm not sure what happened, but he hit me with a toy. Grandpa took him quietly out of church to explain to him that he shouldn't have done that, and he wanted "D," as we call him, to apologize. So Stan quietly walked back in so as not to disturb the service in progress, carrying D, and as he approached the pew, D called out in a loud voice, "Sorry Grandma," and the whole church chuckled.

Kai Lynn, our youngest granddaughter, was about three when she had come to our home in Fort Langley for a visit. It wasn't long before she was asking for her "who, who." What on earth is a "who, who," we wondered, so we looked everywhere with her, upstairs and down. By now she was crying, because we couldn't find whatever it was we were looking for. It wasn't until her next visit that she came happily up the stairs because she had found her "who, who." It turned out to be a mouth organ. I guess she blew "who, who" into it to make music!

Kari Lee and her three – Dionte, Logan, and Kai Lynn sitting on the dock

Logan, our second grandchild, was again about four, and we were on the little ferry from Fort Langley to Maple Ridge, a ride of about five minutes. While we were sailing along, he said, "Grandma, I have to go potty." I said we would have to wait until we got off the ferry as there was no bathroom for the public. So we unloaded from the ferry, and I had forgotten about his need and was driving along the busy Lougheed Highway when he called out from his car seat behind me, "Grandma, I have to go potty." I said I would find a place to pull over but I couldn't find an appropriate place to stop. It wasn't long before he said again, this time a little higher pitch and urgency in his voice, "Grandma, I have to go potty," and I desperately tried to find a place to pull the car over when he said in a weepy little voice, "Grandma, the potty's coming out!" We've had quite a few laughs about that and Logan, as I write, is 14 years old and gave me permission to tell this story.

Another time, Kai Lynn again between two and three was sitting with me one Friday morning on her living room couch. Every Friday, I went over to their home in Maple Ridge to watch the kids. We had just finished our "Grandma eggs," which were simple soft-boiled eggs still in their shell, placed in an egg cup and eaten by scooping the contents out with a spoon. As children, eating eggs in this manner was a normal part of our lives, but over the years was not common. She called them "Grandma eggs" and requested them every Friday morning. This morning after our eggs were eaten and breakfast finished, she got off the couch and stood by my knees facing me. She took her tiny little two-year-old finger and removed some tiny spot from my chin and then stood there by me and asked, "Grandma......uh..... uh......... Grandma..........uh....uh....do....do....uh....do....(I waited patiently through a few more uhs)..... do....uh....do....you....do.....you have a neck?" I couldn't help but laugh. I'm not sure if she couldn't think of the word, or possibly there was some question as to whether or not I did have a neck!

Todd, our second son, was three and a half when his sister was born. I had the baby carriage all ready and comfortable waiting for the baby to come home from the hospital as she had to stay in a few days longer for tests. It turned out to be simply jaundice, but they weren't sure. My mother was staying with me watching the boys, while I went up to the hospital at least once a day. One of those mornings, three-and-a-half-year-old Todd said, "Mom, why don't you and I get into the carriage and Grandma can push." I looked over at Mom who by now was in her 70s, and she looked a bit miffed that somehow she had been delegated to pushing the carriage rather than being in it with us. Mom in her elegance and considering that maybe at her age should be treated with more deference apparently was not impressed. I guess the reaction on Mom's part is what made it seem funny.

Another time when he was just a toddler sitting in his high chair waiting for lunch, I put a spoonful of veggies up to feed him but he wouldn't open his lips. Veggies simply weren't as good as applesauce. So after a couple of attempts I gently put my fingers over his nose and his mouth popped open and in went the vegetables. The next round the same thing – closed lips, finger over the nose and in went the veggies. The third round when the spoonful of veggies approached his lips he put his own little hand over his nose and his mouth popped open and all the veggies went down the little red hatch!

I'd play games with the kids sometimes when looking after them on Fridays, and the neighborhood children would join in. One day I played an old game we played at parties when I was young at Esperanza. You placed eggs on the ground and told the kids they were going to be blindfolded and they had to walk carefully over the eggs but not break them. So I blindfolded them one at a time and replaced the eggs with crackers. They very reluctantly tried stepping over and around the eggs and would hear a crack (of crackers) and be quite anxious. With their arms outspread, they did their best to miss the eggs, which of course they couldn't see. When they were done, we removed the blindfold, and they realized that we had removed the eggs and the cracking they heard was actually soda crackers rather than eggs. The funny part was that they wanted to do it over and over, which of course the effect would not be the same, now that they knew the secret.

Often, I would bake with the children. Sometimes bread or buns. Occasionally, the neighborhood kids would join in. When they were done, they would take their buns home. I always wanted the kids to do something useful and constructive, rather than spending too much time on the phone. One time apparently, Logan, now 12, had his friend over, and I guess I made bread with them. He told me later, he was looking forward to playing with this girlfriend he'd brought along but no, Grandma had her bread-baking project on again!

D, our daughter's oldest boy, was again around three. The family was over for dinner and just before we sat down, I said to my daughter, "Should D have milk or p-o-p?" spelling it out so he wouldn't know. D piped up and said, "I'd like p-o-p!" We couldn't get anything over on him even at three!

My older sister used to tell about a time when I was toddling around. She and Mom were in the kitchen as I made my way into the bedroom. On the way, I saw that the corner of the rug was turned over, so I bent over in my unstable way and straightened it out and continued on my journey. They got a bang out of it, as my Dad used to say, so they thought they'd try it again. They flipped over the corner of the rug again and sure enough I noticed it on the way back and toddled over to it to straighten it up.

Logan was at the crawling stage when he was being cared for by one of my daughter's friends. He apparently was very unhappy, so Kari Lee called to see if I could go and rescue him. I made my way over and knocked on the door. The babysitter opened it and there was little Logan standing in a playpen sobbing. When he saw me, his little eyes brightened and his arms went up. I was happy to pick him up and snuggle him, and his crying stopped instantly.

Then I remembered something I needed from the car. So I put him down on the floor and went out the door, leaving it open as it was summer, and I'd be back in a moment. Well the crying began all over again, and he cried and crawled out the door and was going to crawl all along the sidewalk if necessary until he got to his grandma. I picked him up and kept him by me until we got home, and he was content once again.

Children bring a lot of joy and happy memories into our lives!

YOU Are God's Plan

One day, driving our grandson to elementary school, I said, "Do you know that God has a plan for your life that no one else can do?" His eyes grew big as he leaned over the back of the front seat with a sense of wonder and inspiration. Yes, and that is true for each of us. No matter your birth circumstances, you are God's creation, and He has a plan for everyone. But the choice is ours. To follow or not.

I volunteered at the hospital for a number of years, and my partner at the desk said after long chats on the subject, "Well, the choice is mine to make." And I said, "Yes, it is. But the consequences are eternal." And that's the problem – if you choose not to follow. It is so serious.

I have felt over the last several years that God is preparing us for His coming. I see intense struggles between doing what's right according to the scripture and following the accepted beliefs and theories of today that are leading people in the wrong direction. We are so saturated in electronics that our whole thinking pattern is formed by that. I wonder how our thinking patterns would be if we spent as much time studying the Word as we do studying the computer.

Are we ready? Am I ready? I remember one day, a week or two before Mom died, she stood by the window and said, "I hope I'm ready" and I sat there looking at her and wondered how she could even wonder that after all the years she had served the Lord faithfully on the West Coast of Vancouver Island. But we all need to be sure we are on God's path and not the acceptable, popular road that is encouraged and even taught in some churches.

The Bible tells us the road is narrow. And few there be that find it. That is frightening – the road is narrow. That doesn't sound very open and caring, but it's God's truth and not ours to decide which way is right.

Someone said it was approximately 2,000 years between creation and the flood, about another 2,000 between the flood and Jesus coming to earth, and it is over 2,000 years since He left earth but promised to come back. Might He be returning soon?

I have often thought about the parable of the prodigal son told in the Bible. He took his inheritance and ran. It wasn't long before it was all used up, and he ended up eating out of a pig's trough. If you read carefully, it says that nobody helped him. I've often wondered if he would have ever come back and repented and asked forgiveness if he had someone sympathizing and feeding and caring for him and showing him endless kindness. That would certainly seem like the most loving thing you could do. But sometimes we need to experience the outcome of our choices so that we will change and make better ones.

It takes wisdom to know when to step in to help and when to step back and let our choices work themselves out into lessons learned. There is no other place than God to receive that kind of wisdom. It doesn't come from seeing what other people say is right on the internet. It is not the kind of wisdom popular today. And it takes courage to enact it as it very likely wouldn't be an acceptable decision in today's mixed up thinking.

Many folks continue on the wide road because they are supported in their error. The ones pampering think they are simply loving them. What they are actually doing is keeping them on the wrong road. Are we keeping folks on the wrong path by our silence in the face of wrongdoing? Will the Lord hold us accountable for them? Or are we helping them to see and overcome those things that are wrong?

Wisdom is knowing not what's GOOD to do but what's BEST to do. There are many good things we can do, but they are not always the wisest.

Matthew 7 tells of wonderful folks who spent their lives doing all sorts of miracles and wonderful things in the name of Jesus, but He says to them, "Depart from me. *You disregarded My commands.*" They were doing good things. They were doing loving things. But they weren't doing the things God had told them to do.

Our pastor told a story one day of his flight to attend his grandmother's funeral. As he boarded the plane, he was sombre and just wanted to spend the time on his computer reading, praying, and preparing for the service. He sat down and politely greeted the man beside him and then proceeded to put on his headphones and begin his work. Before long, the man asked a question. The pastor answered shortly and politely and resumed his work. Another question was posed with some revelations of this man's life. And then he ordered a drink that the stewardess brought. Little by little, the conversation became somewhat revealing of a life in question. It wasn't long before the man asked the pastor what he did for a living, and the pastor said, "I think I'm your worst nightmare. I'm a pastor." Well, with a few more drinks and the conversation getting a little rough, our pastor was glad to be landing. He wanted to be one of the first off, so he unbuckled his seat belt and with a polite goodbye headed to the door of the plane. But just before he managed to escape, this by now drunken passenger shouted across the other passengers, "So you think I'm going to hell?" A little taken back but knowing he must be honest, the pastor said, "Yes, if you don't believe in Jesus," and all the other passengers on the plane also received the message.

If you aren't a follower of Christ you can be. It's open for everyone. God loves you. He sent His Son Jesus to earth to tell us about Him, to die for our sins so that we don't have to. The Bible gives us hundreds of years of proof. Jesus did thousands of miracles to prove who He was. He died. And rose up from the grave – proof of His divineness. If you want to be a follower you need to believe this, turn away from a sinful life and walk according to His way outlined in the Bible. It is a sacrifice of our own desires. But it is wonderful! Jesus walks with you all through life. And then your home will be heaven when you leave this earth. It is your choice. I hope you choose to follow Him.

"I Will Carry You"

There's a promise in Isaiah that says, "I have made you and I will carry you." And God certainly was with our parents on the coast, carrying them every step of the way. We have been blessed to be a small part of their lives, and because of their faithfulness, we too have been blessed. I see some of those same qualities of Mom and Dad coming out in our grandchildren, and I wonder, has God called them to some special task? Will they follow? Because it is a choice to obey.

Some of the older members of our family came as staff to Esperanza. Some of us simply grew up there under the influence of the mission. As a child, life on the coast seemed normal to us, but in later years we realized that it was indeed a unique way to grow up.

Mom and Dad loved and cared for the coastal people whether First Nations or white. Always the concern was for their spiritual needs, and physical as well. On the side of our boat, the *Bruce*, was inscribed, "To Preach Christ and Heal Diseases," and everywhere Dad went he did both. He wasn't always appreciated by the loggers and rough people of the company towns, but they sure changed their mind when he prayed over them before they were put to sleep under anesthetic if they required surgery.

The Catholic priests of the Indigenous villages didn't appreciate him either as their messages differed greatly, even though they appeared to follow the same Holy Book, the Bible. The priests discouraged the village folk from coming to the hospital because of the difference in their beliefs and teachings. They also threatened the Natives with taking away their children if they disobeyed them and the Natives were afraid of that. But Dad never did such things and always had their best interest at heart and treated the Natives and even the priests with loving care if they came to him in need.

I have often wondered over the years, in the grand scheme of things, if God had ordained that in the last few hundred years of life on earth that North America was preserved to play out His plan. Europe and the rest of the world were saturated with people, and the world needed a place to grow and thrive. Could it be that God led the explorers to America to bless those who already lived here by crossing the land bridge hundreds of years earlier? Did God want to bring the news of salvation to them? Did He send those folks to establish schools, medical advancements, and the many blessings that came along with that? Surely God has a plan, and the whole coming to America was part of it. After all, this is His world, and He is involved in each detail.

When my father went out into the woods of the interior around Bella Coola, he went with the desire to help those first peoples who were suffering with medical ailments. At first, they did not want to go to the hospitals for treatment. It was all so new and scary for them. But the medical folks tried to convince them that they had new treatments that would ease their pain and condition, and after some time, they acquiesced and truly benefited from the treatments. Dad didn't try to eliminate their language or culture unless he saw it as detrimental to their spiritual needs. He offered them medical advice that would help with general health. He genuinely cared for their physical and spiritual needs, and it was a benefit to them.

I wonder if we should accept God's calling to this wonderful land called North America. Should we understand this coming here as His way to meet the needs of the population of the world and bring the Good News to the folks already here, in the last days of time on earth? His plan is always perfect even though worked out by imperfect people, but His people nonetheless. Mom and Dad were called by God to serve the people of the West Coast. They had a small part in God's plan to bring the Good News to them.

Sometimes, we are called to a great mission. Other times, our calling seems less important. But whatever, it is our obedience to be and do what He calls us to do. Whichever it is, it is all important. I often say, God needs doorknobs too. What would we do without doorknobs? They are important.

They are essential for access to the whole house, but definitely not the center of attention.

Remembering David in the Old Testament, when Samuel came to choose a king from David's family, all the important members were there to be inspected and considered for kingship. But they were not the ones God wanted. They were brought before him one by one to see which one the Lord meant for king. There must be another, Samuel said. Well, there is David, just David. He's out with the sheep. It couldn't be him. But when David was brought in, he was the one chosen by God to be the king. The seeming importance of our position in life is not the important factor. It is our obedience to His calling.

God has a plan for each life. And you are part of it. It always entails sacrifice. Mom didn't want to go to the West Coast, but she willingly went and supported Dad for all 37 years in the isolation of the ministry. His plan is sometimes difficult, but it is always blessed. He is always with those who are His. And He will be with anyone who wants to belong to Him and walk His way.

Not long ago, I was awakened suddenly at five in the morning. I popped up quickly and sat on the edge of my bed, and I knew the Lord was speaking to me through a song. I knew it was a warning that something was coming but that I should trust in His care. The words of this song remind me of home, on the waters of the coast, of the dangers and, yes, even the occasional disasters. Whichever comes our way, the truth is there:

> Fear thou not for I am with thee.
> I will still thy Pilot be.
> Never mind the tossing billows,
> Take My hand, and ***Trust in Me.***

Our home. The trees we tied the bridge to in storms

The view from our home and the hospital. It is Nootka Island.

Miss Parry, the hospital cook, on a busy day prepping trays for the patients.

Mrs. Manning, the post mistress. She sometimes did the hospital laundry.

Printed in Canada